THE Writer's HANDBOOK

by

JANICE L. GORN, Ph. D.

Professor Emerita of Interdisciplinary Studies
New York University

MONARCH PRESS

Contains material previously published in STYLE GUIDE

Copyright © 1973, 1984 by
SIMON & SCHUSTER, INC.

All rights reserved. No part of this book may be reproduced in any form without permission in writing from the publisher.

Published by
MONARCH PRESS
A Division of Simon & Schuster, Inc.
Simon & Schuster Building
1230 Avenue of the Americas
New York, N.Y. 10020
MONARCH PRESS and colophon are registered trademarks of Simon & Schuster, Inc.
Library of Congress Catalog Card Number: 83-63364
Standard Book Number: 0-671-50424-X

10 9 8 7 6 5 4 3 2 1

Printed in the United States of America

Foreword

The writer is deeply indebted to those generous and loving men and women who, formally and informally, served as her teachers. By precept and example, they helped her to develop the procedures and the rigorous discipline necessary to respectable research. They cultivated her appreciation for elegance and economy in the writing of others and in her own literary efforts. Association with them taught her the invaluable quality of humor, the skill to laugh at herself, and a proper humility. They nurtured her sense of wonder and her passion for beauty and knowledge. Those great teachers are: Geoffrey Bruun, Esmond S. de Beer, Emilie Joseph Jacoby, Morris Jacoby, Frederick Lehmann, Walter MacKellar, Adolphe E. Meyer, John C. Payne, William Shakespeare, and Marshall J. Tyree.

—Janice L. Gorn

Introduction

This book is meant for the person who, by force of circumstance, must write, as well as for the person who wishes to write, and for the person who is compelled to write by some inexplicable power which cannot be denied. This writer has assumed that, with the exception of those persons afflicted with insurmountable physical, mental or emotional disabilities, everyone can write.

Whether writing for fun, or because one is obsessed with an idea, or because one has been given an assignment, or because one must write to obtain advancement, there are a few minimal requisites. The reader should expect and find: clarity and correctness in grammar, diction and spelling. In addition, whether a brief essay, a vignette, a term paper, or a full-length history or novel, the writer has responsibility for presenting a work that in organization, form and, where appropriate, documentation will be comprehensible to an intelligent, literate reader.

The rules presented in this book are not meant to be irrevocable. Schools, colleges, universities, publishers frequently have their own strictures for the presentation of written work. For obvious reasons, it may be necessary to bend to such demands.

If the reader has problems of documentation,[i] subject development or style to which he[ii] can find no answers, or if he has other difficulties with this *Handbook* please write:

> Professor Janice L. Gorn
> New York University
> East Building — Room 320
> New York, N.Y. 10003

Include your name, address, position or school, and any other information about the problem or problems with which you need help.

---

[i] Lower-case Roman numerals (i,ii,iii, etc.) are used for footnotes to the text of this book. Arabic numerals (1, 2, 3, etc.) are the appropriate symbols. To avoid confusion, they have been reserved for footnote examples in the body of the text.

[ii] Masculine pronouns will be used throughout this work unless inappropriate. If not otherwise indicated, it is to be assumed that all statements apply as well to the feminine.

Contents

	FOREWORD	iii
	INTRODUCTION	v
I	PROPHYLAXIS OR HOW TO AVOID DISASTERS	1
	The Topic	1
	Copyright Laws	1
	Taking Notes	2
	Note Cards	3
	Library Information	3
	Direct Quotations	4
	Plagiarism	4
	Mechanical Preparation	5
	Discrepancies	5
	Index	6
II	USAGE	7
	Poor Usage	7
	Unnecessary Words	7
	"I," "My," and "We"	8
	"Feel" and "Think"	8
	Paragraph Structure	8
	Sentence Structure	8
	Diction	9
	Spelling	13
	Capitalization and Titles	13
	Punctuation	14
	Colon before a Quotation	14
	Single Quotation Marks	15
	Minor Series	15
	Major Series	15
	Parenthetical Remarks	15
	Numbers and Punctuation	16
	Numbers and Numerals	17

Symbols	17
Italics	17
Material in a Language Other Than English	17
The Addition of Italics	18
Abbreviations	18
Primary Citation of a Person in the Text	19
The Use of Abstracts, Digests, and Syntheses	19

III FORMAT 21

Paper	21
Margins	21
Pagination	21
Copyright Symbol	22
Spacing	22
Heads and Subheads	23
Levels of Subheads	23
Quotations, Quotation Marks and Ellipses	24
Quotation within a Quotation	24
Ellipses in a Quotation	25
Incomplete Sentence in a Quotation	25
Insert in a Quotation	26
The Superior Number	26
Citation of Poetry	27
Typing Dialogue	28

IV DOCUMENTATION THROUGH FOOTNOTES 30

Enumeration of Footnotes	30
Spacing in Footnotes	30
Placement in Footnotes	31
Sample Footnotes	31
Footnote for an Article	31
Footnote for a Book	32
Footnote for a Chapter in a Book or an Essay in a Collection of Essays	32
Documenting the Classics	34
Footnote for a Dissertation, Master's Thesis, Mimeographed Paper	35
Legal Documentation	36
Documentation for Paraphrase	37
Place of Publication	37
Documenting within a Chapter	38
Repeated Citations of the Same Work	38
Multiple Authors or Editors	38
Organization As Author	39
Missing Information	39

	Ibid.	40
	Personal Communication: Interview, Letter, Telephone Call	41
	Lecture Notes	41
	Newspaper Articles	42
	Volumes, Editions, Revisions	42
	Books by One Author, Revised by Another	43
	Citation of Reissued Books	43
	Documentation through Footnotes: A Summary	44
V	BIBLIOGRAPHY	45
	Bibliographic Classification	45
	Spacing and Indenting the Bibliography	46
	Bibliographic Entries	46
	Sequence of Bibliographic Entry of a Book	46
	Sequence of Bibliographic Entry of Essay, Article, etc.	47
	Sequence of Bibliographic Entry of More Than One Book by the Same Author	48
	Citing from a Compilation or Anthology	48
	Citing Multiple Authors	48
	Sample Bibliography	49
	Special Bibliographic Lists	52
VI	TABLES, FIGURES, CHARTS, GRAPHS, ILLUSTRATIONS	53
	Appropriate Use	53
	Tables	54
	Reduction of Tables, Charts, Graphs	56
	Figures and Illustrations	58
	Reduction of Illustrations	61
VII	THE TERM PAPER	62
	The Teacher, The Topic and You	62
	Procedures	64
	The Title	64
	The Descriptive Sentence or Paragraph	65
	The Work Plan	65
	First Term Paper Topic	66
	Search of the Card Files	66
	Second Term Paper Topic	67
	Taking Notes	68
	The Outline	69
	Writing the Paper	70
	Opening Paragraph	70

	First Draft	70
	Second Draft	71
	Concluding Section	72
	Final Copy	72
VIII	THE DOCTORAL DISSERTATION AND THE MASTER'S THESIS	74
	The Subject and You	74
	Choosing a Topic	75
	Scope of the Research	77
	Selecting a Sponsor	78
	The Dissertation Proposal	79
	The Statement of the Problem	79
	The Subproblems	80
	Definitions	80
	Limitations	81
	Hypotheses	82
	The Need for the Study	83
	Related Literature	83
	The Method	85
	Bibliography	86
	Appendixes	87
	Curriculum Vitae	87
	Title	87
	Sample Catalogue for Dissertation Proposal	87
	Onward and Upward	88
IX	FOREIGN WORDS AND ABBREVIATIONS	89
	Words in Other Languages	89
	Abbreviations Lists	92
X	FOREWORD, ACKNOWLEDGMENTS, TABLE OF CONTENTS, ABBREVIATIONS	93
	Foreword	93
	Acknowledgments	93
	Table of Contents	94
	Abbreviations	94
	Sample Table of Contents	94
	APPENDIXES	96
	A. Singular and Plural Forms	96
	B. Books on Usage and Useful Books	97
	INDEX	99

CHAPTER I
Prophylaxis or How to Avoid Disasters

The Topic

It does not make any difference whether you are writing a letter of reference for a friend or what you hope will be a best-selling novel. You had better know what you are talking about. It is the considered opinion of writers, editors and critics that, unless you are that very rare person — a creative genius — trying to write about a subject which is unknown or even slightly known to you can lead only to failure.

Every now and then one is forced to write on a subject which one does not know or to which one is violently antipathetic. The paper may be an assignment by a teacher. If there is no way to avoid the task, do everything possible to learn as much as you can within the time provided and do even more to avoid letting your prejudice intervene between you and a respectable piece of writing. It isn't easy — try!

If the choice of topic is yours, try to select one with which you are comfortable or, better still, about which you are enthusiastic. Do not rely on what you *think* you know about it. Try to improve your knowledge of it by making use of people who are deemed to be experts and by spending as much time as possible on research. That applies to any subject, even if you believe you are an expert. There is always someone who knows more about the subject or about matters related to the subject. You may think it unlikely, but it is possible to develop real enthusiasm for a subject if you have explored it thoroughly.[i]

Copyright Laws

Anything you write which will be distributed, in no matter how limited

---
[i] For a more extensive discussion of assigned writing, see Chapter VII, 62–73.

a fashion, beyond the confines of a classroom or a select group of friends, is subject to copyright laws. Term papers, private documents within an institution and personal letters are *not* required to adhere to those laws. Writers of published articles, books, Masters' theses and doctoral dissertations are bound to respect national and international copyright regulations.[i]

Before you make use of any part of a published work, be sure to look at the copyright page, usually positioned on the back of the title page of a book. Many authors hold their own copyrights. Should you need permission to quote, it is to the copyright holder or the publisher you must turn. Check also whether there are two editions of the book, *e.g.*, British and American. If so you may have to contact both publishers. However, if the symbol © is present, the book is covered by International Copyright agreement and permission from one source covers all who are parties to that contract.

Taking Notes

You may have been seeking a particular article for a very long time and the day finally comes when you lay hands on the journal, brochure, book or microfiche which you have been tracking down for weeks. Restrain yourself! Do not start to read immediately. Take down *all* of the information you might need for documenting your sources, *i.e.*, for footnotes and for bibliography.

For an article, note the first and last pages. If the article is not sequentially paginated, make note of *all* the pages. For example, *Scientific American* interlards advertisements: you might need to record pages 3–8, 12, 22–23. After you have all of the information, read the article, chapter or brochure. If it is of no use to you, make a written note as to why it is not pertinent. This will prevent you from reading it again should someone suggest that you do so or ask you why you have not made mention of it. Your note may avert a useless trip to the library.

All of the information cited for an article is also needed for a brochure, a monograph or a leaflet. If you are about to read a book or one chapter therein, the same caution is necessary. Record the title of the book, *all* of the authors, the place of publication, the publisher, and the date of publication, the first and last pages of a chapter, if that is the object of your interest. If you are using a collection of essays by different authors, note the name of the author of the chapter you think relevant to your writing. Differentiate in your notes between those persons whose names appear on the title page, who may be editors, and the persons who contributed the individual chapters.

Check everything you read for a copyright notice. Some authors hold

---

[i] Information is available from Copyright Office, Library of Congress, Washington, D.C., 20540. Make requests for the specific information you need.

copyrights on *all* of their published work—articles as well as books. Some magazines print the copyright notice perpendicular to the text at the outer margin. If no author's copyright notice is found, the publisher of the work must be assumed to hold the copyright.

Note Cards

You may be comfortable with or addicted to yellow legal pads or looseleaf notebooks. They may be fine for shopping lists, but they are poor for taking notes: the paper curls, it is hard to stuff into a pocket or pocketbook, it is difficult to file. Large pieces of paper simply do not handle easily.

Cards! If you have small hands, stick to 3" x 5" or, better, 4" x 6". The best, if you can manage them, are 5" x 8". Establish a cataloguing system. If your topic appears at the outset to have three themes, start with them. Eventually, you may have forty or fifty categories. *Never* use the back of a card! You may forget that you've done so and frantically look for the important information you appear to have lost. If your notes on one piece of material require more than one card, number each one and repeat the title at the top. That way, if you are using more than one article or essay by the same author, there will be less chance of confusion. If you have notes which appear to be applicable to more than one of your categories, cross reference. As in the illustration, you might use "X" in the upper left corner to indicate cross reference.

Plato 1	X Art and Artists
Randall, John Herman, Jr.	See Plato, Randall, John
"Plato As the Philosopher of	Herman, Jr. "Plato As the
the Artistic Experience,"	Philosopher of the Artistic
The American Scholar,	Experience."
Summer 1968, 37:3, 2-12.	
Notes	

Library Information

Some libraries are equipped with computer retrieval systems for their own holdings, as well as terminals connecting them to a variety of other libraries and information sources. Some libraries are in the process of acquiring facilitating devices and some libraries, for lack of funds, are forced to make the best of their old equipment. The same conditions prevail with the numerical identification of books, journals, etc. Many libraries are still using the Dewey decimal system; some libraries are in the transitional stage switching to Library of Congress identification; and some libraries have completely revised their systems.

Note on your card whatever identifying number is present and the library in which you used the particular material. Then, if you must return to the library, your time will be spent in reading, not in tracking down the way to find what you need.

Direct Quotations

When copying direct quotations, regardless of the source, if the quotation starts on one page and continues on another, be sure to note the page number after the last word appearing on the first of the two pages. If copying several pages, do the same thing for each page. Do *NOT* use those numbers in the final manuscript. They are for your use only.

Example

We came to Suva in the Fiji islands on a Sunday morning. From every direction, one could see families walking toward town to attend church. Women wore long white translucent skirts with full dresses as blouses; men wore dark skirts, just below the knee in length; en- [92] chanting-looking boys in white wrap-around skirts were kicking stones along the way. 93

Why? Because everything looks priceless, magnificent — in the library. When you are writing, you may find that you want to stop at "blouses." If you had omitted the notation of [92] and just entered 92–93 at the end of the quotation, back to the library you would have to go. Too often, the book is out and its return date is not predictable.

If you plan to paraphrase the quotation, note each page on which the excerpt you will be putting in your own words appears. You will then know on which page each idea appeared. A paraphrase requires exactly the same documentation as a direct quotation.

While you are in the white heat of copious note-taking, try to accommodate yourself to the idea that you will not be using all of these deathless gems. Strenuously resist the temptation to use a reproducing machine to copy everything you see. Read carefully and take notes only on what seems directly related to your topic. The frenzy to reproduce is costly in time and money.

In the final writing, no matter what the topic, one of the criteria for judgment of your competence will be your power to discriminate between what is and what is not pertinent. Be prepared to file from 50% to 90% of the notes you so painfully acquired. Do not grieve! Most of those notes really were not so remarkable, and the remainder may make good references for articles and speeches.

Plagiarism

There are few things an author may do which elicit the total condemnation that stealing the work of someone else invariably produces. Under no circumstances may one be exonerated for using the creative work of another person and claiming it as one's own. Whether it be a very small theft or a large one, it is unforgivable. Using someone else's idea or using his words, *i.e.*, expressing his idea in your own words (paraphrasing), or using his exact words (direct quotations), or altering his words slightly, each such appropriation of the possession or product of someone else requires documentation in a footnote. To add force to this statement, bear in mind that plagiarism may be punished by a monetary fine, imprisonment or both.

Mechanical Preparation

If you are a capable typist, it would be well if you typed the work yourself. If you are not the best, but are able to type, it is advisable for you to prepare the material for a professional typist. The typist is *not* obligated to correct your errors in writing or in documentation. It is your work and you are responsible for *all* of it. If you cannot type, but have a legible handwriting, even that is better than handing a typist a mass of raggle-taggle notes.

The most modern typewriters make it possible to change type faces and to justify right margins (make them even). If that form of machine is not available to you, you will have to make do with what is.

Word processors[i] are wonderful devices, but they are not appropriate for someone who cannot handle a typewriter. If you envision a life of writing and plan to buy one, try to rent one or use a friend's. Be patient for it takes a while to accommodate to a new procedure. If you have taken time to adjust and find that you cannot, don't buy one. Also, test a number of machines until you find one that will do what you need. The manufacturer can provide many adaptations; don't settle for something that costs so much, but does not meet your needs.

Discrepancies

From time to time, you may find entries under examples, or footnote displays, or bibliographic items which appear to be in opposition to rules stated in this text. In almost every instance, these seeming discrepant matters are a consequence of a rule which takes precedence over all other rules. Whenever possible, do *not* tamper with what someone else has written or with the printed word. The major exception to that over-arching rule would be a gross error on the part of the writer or printer. Even in that case, you would use the writer's or printer's words, but you would call attention to the error by making use of the standard device, *i.e.*, *sic.*[ii]

---

[i] See William Zinsser, *Writing with a Word Processor,* New York: Harper & Row, 1983.
[ii] See Chapter IX, text and n.i. 91.

Index

Consult the index of any book you are reading. That applies, of course, to this book. It is provided to assist you in finding the particular passage or section for which you have need. It may save you great quantities of time which you might have wasted in being forced to read a considerable number of pages of narrative of no consequence to your objective.

CHAPTER II

Usage

Poor Usage

The tendency to attempt to make a topic "significant" by drowning it in verbiage must be avoided. Good writing requires direct expression — that is, the use of words to communicate clearly. Do not be ostentatious or extravagant; save words.

Unnecessary Words

Note how the expressions in the left-hand column below can be reduced or slimmed down to the shorter, clearer forms in the right-hand column:

1. "at this time" — "now"
2. "due to the fact that" — "because"
3. "concerning the matter of" — "about"
4. "in reference to" — "on" or "about"
5. "for the purpose of" — "to"
6. "as of this date" — "yet"
7. "during the course of" — "during"
8. "in the event of" — "if"
9. "in view of the fact that" — "since" or "because"
10. "despite the fact that" — "although"

There are also words that are useless, annoying, and repetitious. Note the unnecessary words underscored below.

1. "These are the true facts."
2. "Would you repeat that again?"
3. "We must not neglect the vital, modern issues of today."

Sometimes a short word is more effective than a long one. You may "use" a method quite legitimately. You do not have to "utilize" it. And most of the time what you mean is "method," not "methodology."

There are "subjects." "Subject content areas" is a hideous mixture of English, information, and geography. More is not necessarily better; "subject matter" is no more explicit or helpful than "subject."

There is "behavior." It takes many forms, and, of recent date, each has acquired its own little name; "behaviors" is an easy out! So is "learnings."

"I," "My," and "We"

Depending upon the whim of your professor, you may —or may not— use "I" or "my" in a term paper. You may *not* use either in a Master's thesis or a doctoral dissertation; "the candidate," "the researcher," "the investigator," "his research," "her findings," etc., are acceptable. "We" is also unacceptable, except in the case of a group project.

"Feel" and "Think"

Don't use "feel" when what is needed is "think." It is not the word "feel" alone that gives one pause; it is the sentimental, bathetic quality it implies. "Feeling" about poverty, deprivation, violence, *et al.*, may very well evoke tears in you; "thinking" about them and exploring the thoughts of responsible scholars about them might just yield a solution. Avoid "feel"; do try to "think."

Paragraph Structure

A paragraph is a major unit of thought. One should indent only five spaces to indicate a paragraph, unless specific regulations require otherwise. The first sentence of a paragraph may be a presentation of the topic or a bridge between the thought in the preceding paragraph and the thought to be presented within the new paragraph. Each sentence which follows the opening sentence should contribute to the orderly development of the topic. When a paragraph encompasses the entire topic, the closing sentence should summarize or emphasize the central thought of the paragraph.

Sentence Structure

Unless a sentence is, in fact, an exclamation rather than a true sentence — *e.g.*, "What a bore!" — it should have a subject and a verb.

Economy in writing is a virtue! Excessively long or complex sentences discourage the reader. Oversimplification is tedious and childlike. The happy medium is desirable. Parenthetical remarks should be used sparingly. No paragraph should consist of one interminable sentence. A sentence which engulfs an entire page may be necessary when you write a first draft for your eyes alone. It should be carefully edited before subjecting any other human being to such verbal effluvia. The eye resists and the mind boggles when confronted with so undisciplined an avalanche of words. It is no longer possible to call Georg Wilhelm Friedrich Hegel or John Dewey to task for such behavior, but you are not in their advantaged position.

Diction

Extend yourself to select the word which most precisely suits your purposes and most accurately expresses the meaning you wish to convey. Do not strive to use a word or words which, because obscure, you believe to be scholarly. At all times, your primary concern is the one best word for communicating your meaning.

The following word guide, or *glossary*, reviews some of the words that cause constant trouble. Study this glossary and apply the insights it provides for better speaking and writing.

accept, except *Accept* means *to receive; except* when used as a verb means *to exclude. We accepted the new program. Tom's name was excepted from the committee roster.* The word *except* is used most often as a preposition. *Everyone went except me.*

affect, effect The verb *affect* means *to influence.* The verb *effect* means *to bring about.* The noun *effect* means result. *The Dean's decision did not affect the program. The new program will effect many changes. The new program will have a good effect on student morale.*

aggravate The verb *aggravate* means *to intensify* or *increase* when used formally. *The rain aggravated their suffering.* Many use the word *aggravate* also to mean *to irritate* or *to annoy.* This latter usage should be avoided.

already, all ready *Already* means *before* or *by a certain time; all ready* means *fully, completely,* or *entirely ready. Mike said that he had already received his voucher. When the whistle blew, the girls were all ready for the game.*

all right, alright Always spell this expression *all right.*

altogether, all together *Altogether* means *completely, entirely, wholly; all together* means *as a group. We find Peggy altogether too conceited. After the explosion, the foreman was relieved to find his group all together in front of the building.*

among, between *Among* applies to *three or more; between* applies to *two. He divided the commission evenly among the three college students. He divided the commission evenly between the two college students.* Occasionally, the word *between* is used with three or more if a give-and-take situation results or a point in a relationship is established. *The cotton triangle required cooperation between the South, the Northeast, and England. Columbus proved to be the most convenient point between Cleveland, Cincinnati, and Toledo.*

amount, number *Amount* applies to *bulk, mass,* or *quantity; number* applies to *a quantity that can be counted.* There is a larger amount of snow on the lawn today than there was yesterday. A large number of these books is available in the bookstore.

as, as a means of, as a method of, as to The conjunction *as* provides a useful connective, but it sometimes leads to loose, flabby structures. Do not use *as* when you mean *that* or *whether.* I am not certain that (not *as*) he will bring the road map. I am not certain whether (not *as*) he wrote. Avoid the indirect expressions *as a means of* and *as a method of* when you mean *for.* You will find walking useful for (not *as a means of* or *as a method of*) reducing nervous tension. Do not use *as to* for *about.* He requested information about (not *as to*) your article on wasps.

being as, being that Do not use these illiteracies for *since* or *that.*

beside, besides *Beside* means *alongside of; besides* means *in addition to.* They sat beside the brook all afternoon. Besides, Tom doesn't want the job.

between, among See **among, between.**

but that, but what Do not use in place of *that* in structures like *I do not question that* (not *but that*) *you are faster.*

center around It is not possible to *center around.* You may *revolve about* or *around* and you may *circumnavigate.* But you must *center on.*

continual, continuous *Continual* applies to a *succession that is steady but broken from time to time; continuous* applies to an *unbroken succession.* The space flight was guided by continual corrections from Houston. The mud was washed away by the continuous rain from Monday through Wednesday.

could of Do not use for *could have*

data *Data* is the plural of *datum. Data are gathered.* Say *these data* rather than *this data.*

deal Do not use this colloquial term for *arrangement* or *transaction* in formal expression. He enjoys an excellent arrangement (not *deal*) with the business manager of the State College Journal.

different from, different than Prefer idiomatic *different from.*

effect, affect See **affect, effect**

equally as good Prefer *equally good.*

except, accept See **accept, except**

expect Do not use this word when you mean *believe, suppose,* or *think.* I do not think (not *expect*) that the postman has been here.

farther, further *Farther* applies to *distance in space; further* applies to *additional* or *advanced degrees* or *quantities.* We walked farther east than we did south. The mayor waited for further information.

fewer, less *Fewer* applies to *quantities that can be counted; less* applies to *quantities that must be measured rather than counted.* Observe these distinctions in all formal expression. *Our team made fewer errors and displayed less confusion than any other team in the tournament.*

focus around Do not use in place of *focus on.*

former, latter *Former* applies to the *first named in a series of two; latter* refers to the *last named in a series of two.* Do not use *former* to indicate the first of a series of three or more and *latter* to indicate the last of a series of three or more.

if, whether Prefer *whether* to *if* in structures that follow verbs like *ask, doubt, know, learn, say. Henry V did not know whether* (not *if*) *he had won the battle.*

imply, infer Imply means *to hint at an idea without expressing it directly; infer* means *to draw an understanding or conclusion from someone's expression or a situation. The professor implied that the student was not listening carefully. He inferred from Jane's remark that she was bored.*

in, into *In* applies to *something located within something else; into* applies to *a movement from the outside to the inside. John sat in the office. John walked into the office.*

in back of Prefer *at the back of* or *behind.*

infer, imply See **imply, infer**

irregardless Avoid this impropriety. Say *regardless.*

its, it's *Its* is the possessive of *it*; *it's* is the contraction of *it is.*

kind of, sort of Do not use *kind of* and *sort of* as adverbs in formal expression. *Falstaff was quite* (not *kind of* or *sort of*) *witty in Henry IV, Part 1.*

kind of a, sort of a Omit the *a. What kind of* (not *kind of a* or *sort of a*) *wine is Chablis?*

leave, let Avoid the nonstandard *Leave* him go for *Let* him go. The word *leave* means *depart. I leave today.* The word *let* means *to allow. Let me take your place.*

less, fewer See **fewer, less**

like Do not use *like* as a subordinating conjunction in formal expression. *Like* is a preposition when used as a connective: *A writer like Stephen Crane is rare.* Use a subordinating conjunction, not the preposition *like,* in structures like the following: *He tries hard, as* (not *like*) *most players do.*

likely, liable The word *likely* applies to *anything probable;* the word *liable* applies to an *unpleasant possibility,* an *exposure to punishment,* or a *responsibility. You are likely* (not *liable*) *to get the part of François Villon in the play. You are liable to fall off the stage if you get too excited.*

might of Avoid this illiteracy for *might have.*

must of Avoid this illiteracy for *must have.*

myself, himself, yourself These pronouns are to be used as intensives (*The Dean himself will open the conclave*) or as reflexives (*He hit himself when he beat the carpet*). Do not use these forms when *me, him,* or *you* will serve. *We shall be honored if John and you* (not *yourself*) *join us for tea at the Plaza.*

nice Do not use in formal expression for *becoming, pleasant, pretty, winsome. John met an attractive* (not *nice*) *girl at the dance.* The word *nice* means *subtle* or *fine. He made some nice distinctions between Freudian and interpersonal theory.*

number, amount See **amount, number**

off of Omit the *of. The book fell off* (not *off of*) *the shelf.*

per Avoid the pretentious Latin preposition in statements like *per your letter.*

practical, practicable *Practical* applies to *actual use as distinguished from theory; practicable* means *feasible* or *possible. My father is a practical man. The chairman did not consider the program practicable for May.*

principal, principle *Principal* applies to *a chief* or *the chief part of something; principle* applies to *a basic law. Mr. Jones is the principal of the school. Professor White was the principal speaker. He paid both the interest and the principal. Fair play is a good principle to follow.*

reason is because, reason is that Prefer *the reason is that* in formal speaking and writing.

respectfully, respectively *Respectfully* means *with respect,* as in the complimentary close of a letter *respectfully yours; respectively* means that *each item will be considered in the order given. This paper is respectfully submitted. The hero, the heroine, and the villain will be played by Albert, Joan and Harry, respectively.*

said Avoid the legalistic use of *said* like *said letter, said plan, said program* except in legal writing.

should of Do not use for *should have.*

some Do not use *some* when you mean *somewhat.*

sort of, kind of See **kind of, sort of**

sort of a, kind of a See **kind of a, sort of a**

such Do not use *such* as an intensive in formal expression. *My sister has such a wonderful way with children* is permissible in friendly conversation. *My sister has a wonderful way with children* is preferred in formal speaking and writing.

try and Use *try to.*

wait for, wait on *Wait for* means *to await; wait on* means *to serve. I am waiting for* (not *waiting on*) *Tom to call.*

way, ways Do not use *ways* for *way. It is a long way* (not *ways*) *to California.*

where Do not use *where* in place of *that* in expressions like the following: *I see in the newspaper that* (not *where*) *a jet airport will be built near Hampton.*

Spelling

Inaccurate spelling is as insupportable as faulty diction. The usual hackneyed plaint, "I've always been a poor speller," is not tenable. The following list includes words that are commonly misspelled.

Correct	Incorrect
definitely	definately
develop	develope
discernible	disernible
disciples	disiples
discipline	disipline
environment	enviornment
existence	existance
feasible	feasable
in order	inorder
intelligible	intelligable
judgment	judgement
persistent	persistant
privilege	priviledge
tenet	tenant (when *tenet* is meant)
track	tract (when *track* is meant)

Capitalization and Titles

Some words lead a dual existence, *e.g.*, federal; some lead a triple or quadruple existence, *e.g.*, state.

Examples

He was inclined to believe in a *federal* system of government.

She was a representative of the *Federal* Government of Graustark.

The lady of the house was in a distraught *state*.

In doing research on welfare practices, one should examine municipal, *state*, and federal regulations.

It was a *state* occasion, and the mayors of the major cities had not been invited.

He entered a plea to the Department of *State* of the United States.

She lived in the *state* of California.

Similar procedure prevails in the use of other titles, *e.g.*, bishop, king, governor.

Titles of books, journals, newspapers, and monographs are always italicized (underscored). Titles of chapters, articles, and sections of books are placed in quotation marks. All words in titles have initial capitals, with the exception of prepositions and articles, *e.g.*, of, to, from, a, an. The first word of a title is capitalized even if it is an article or a preposition.

Punctuation

Appropriate punctuation may make the difference between clarity and confusion.

Example

Mrs. Hawkins said Mary is a shrew.

"Mrs. Hawkins," said Mary, "is a shrew."

The period, exclamation point, and question mark signal the end of a thought. The comma indicates a minor pause upon the way or the dividing mark within a series. The semicolon indicates a longer pause and the separation of larger ideas, phrases, constructions, or more important identities. The colon indicates that a series of items or ideas will follow.

Colon before a Quotation

When a quotation is used to illustrate or strengthen a point, it should be preceded by a colon if it is a complete sentence or, as in the first illustration, an exclamation, or if it is preceded by a verb, as in the second illustration.

Example

Many expressions have been attributed to him; we quote his exact words: "Death to all tyrants!"

Example

He is known to have said: "Damn the torpedoes!"

If the quotation is being used as an integral part of a sentence, the punctuation should follow established form.

Example

It was a happy occasion in every way "... a delightful excursion into the past."

OR

It was a happy occasion, "... a delightful excursion into the past."

Single Quotation Marks

Sometimes it just seems too complicated to bother!

Example

The title of Gould's column tells the story: "Important Breakthroughs for 'Sesame Street.'"

Minor Series

In a series of more than three short elements, the elements are separated by commas, including a comma before the conjunction joining the last two elements.

Examples

He will be bringing bread and salt.

He will be bringing bread, salt and wine.

He will be bringing bread, salt, a bird, and a bottle.

Major Series

In a series of long or complicated elements, separate the elements with semicolons rather than commas.

> Some of the early theories pertaining to learning are still worthy of attention, Quintilian's view of the relationship between predisposed personality and intellectual attainment; Comenius's child development theory; Rousseau's "punishment by natural consequences" theory; and Herbart's "apperceptive mass."

Parenthetical Remarks

Rule. When a parenthetical remark is a complete sentence, the punctuation is inside the final parenthesis:

There are innumerable interpretations of the personality of Hamlet, both in literary form and in the memory of those privileged to have seen the many productions of the play done in New York in the past 35 years. (Mr. Howard's fits into no one of these categories!)

Rule. When the parenthetical remark is not a complete sentence, the closing parenthesis is followed by the punctuation:

The personality of Hamlet has been variously interpreted by such stellar performers as Gielgud, Evans, Redgrave, and Olivier (not in order of importance), but Howard's defies description.

Rule. If you wish to set an idea off from the main body of a sentence, use a dash [—] before the idea and a dash after the idea.

Malapropisms are inappropriate in scholarly work — sending a girl to a "female cemetery" — except as a deliberate device.

Exception. If the phrase or clause concludes the sentence, place the dash before the concluding phrase or clause.

Professors are expected to be available for consultation every weekday — but don't count on it.

Numbers and Punctuation

Rule. When enumerating a series of ideas, principles, or theories, only one form of punctuation is necessary. Either one of the following examples is correct:

1) The Ionic mode, 2) the Aeolian mode and 3) the Lidian mode...

OR

1. the Mixolidian mode, 2. the Phrygian mode and 3. the Aeolian mode...

Comment. This rule applies to an enumerated series in your own narrative, in quotations within the narrative, or in indented material, either for a quotation or for emphasis.

Rule. In an outline, one *never* uses a numeral — Roman or Arabic — or a letter — capital or lower case — singly. There is no I without a II, no A without a B. The sequence of numbers and letters, with appropriate punctuation, for an outline is as follows:

I. Nature and purpose of the research project
   A. Subject of concern
      1. The child
      2. The environment
         a. The family
         b. The community
            1) The school
            2) Other agencies
               a) Cultural
                  (1) Libraries
                  (2) Museums, theatres, etc.
               b) Political
   B. Method of procedure
II. Content and audience.

Numbers and Numerals

Rule. You may not begin a sentence with a numeral! If a sentence must begin with a number, spell it out.

Rule. Numbers from one to ten should be spelled out; all other numbers may be numerals.

Symbols

In narrative, the words "dollar" and "percent" or "percentage" should be used. In citing amounts of money or percentages, the symbols $ and % should be used.

Italics

Unless you have the use of a typewriter with changeable type faces, it will be necessary to underscore any words, titles, or other materials which would otherwise be in italics. The underscoring indicates to the reader that the material is intended to be italicized.

Material in a Language Other Than English[1]

Citations from works in any language other than English may appear in translation in the text with the original language in a footnote, *or* the procedure may be reversed. *Both* original and translation must be provided. The material in the language other than English should be in italics.

---

[1] See Chapter IX, "Foreign Words and Abbreviations," 89–91.

Cette personne, . . . c'est M. Bold, Ministre de l'église Anglicane, qui a publie quelques Ouvrages en faveur de M. Locke.[1]

[1] "This person is Mr. Bold, minister in the Anglican Church, who has published several pieces in support of Mr. Locke." B.M. Additional M.S. 4222, ff. 255-257.

Rule. A translator other than yourself should be cited in both footnotes and bibliography.

FOOTNOTE

[1] Philip Melancthon, *The School System of Greater Germany*, trans. from 1530 ed. by Herman Reuchlin, Göttingen: Lehmann Press, 1970.

BIBLIOGRAPHY

Melancthon, Philip. *The School System of Greater Germany*, trans. from 1530 ed. by Herman Reuchlin. Göttingen: Lehmann Press, 1970.

Rule. If you are not fluent in the language, consult an expert and give full acknowledgment to him at the outset of your manuscript. If you are doing *all* of the translation, provide a footnote to that effect at the outset of the manuscript. If you are doing *some* of the translation, so stipulate.

[1] In all instances where a published translation was not available, Dr. John Doe, Professor of Romance Languages, Bennington College, has translated from the French and Spanish; Dr. Richard Roe, Professor of Classical Languages, Fordham University, has translated from the Latin and Greek.

[1] All translations, other than those available in published works, and so indicated, have been done by the researcher.

[1] All translations from German, French, Italian, and Latin have been done by the researcher. Translations from the Russian were done by Dr. Boris Goudanov, University of Vilna. Only translators other than the researcher will be cited.

The Addition of Italics

Rule. If you add italics to a quotation, you are obligated to make that clear to the reader.

Example

. . . and it has become increasingly evident that *no one method is appropriate to every child.*[1]

[1] Emilie Joseph, *Teaching Reading Requires Imagination*, San Francisco: Jacobovsky Press, 1906, 10. Italics added.

Abbreviations

When using the names of organizations, standardized tests and titles affixed to theories, spell out the entire name the first time and follow it with the initial letters usually used, *e.g.*, Department of Health, Education and Welfare (HEW). Although the department is defunct, reference to it continues. If there is not a common set of initial letters, devise one, *e.g.*, Hospitalized Veterans of the United States (HVUS), or language laboratory method (LLM). If you are devising the abbreviation, omit periods between the letters. If you are using an established abbreviation, follow the standard. Some abbreviations use periods, some do not. The parenthetical set of letters after the full title means that thereinafter you will be using the abbreviation.

Primary Citation of a Person in the Text

The first time you refer to an authority, author, or consultant, use his or her full name, *e.g.*, *Matthew Cole* or *Francine Silverblank*. Thereafter, use only his or her last name: *Cole* or *Silverblank*.

If there are two authors whose surname is the same, first give the full citation: *Peter Smith* and *John Smith*. Thereafter, refer to them as *P. Smith* and *J. Smith*.

If they are both named Peter Smith, then employ their middle initials: *Peter F. Smith* and *Peter L. Smith*, or *P. F. Smith* and *P. L. Smith*.

If there are no middle initials available, or if by some fluke both authors have identical initials, then you might indicate that the first Smith you cite fully will be identified only as *Smith,* and that any subsequent Smith, after complete citation, will be identified by both his first and last names. Any complication beyond those mentioned will require a little imagination and ingenuity on your part.

The Use of Abstracts, Digests, and Syntheses

Rule. A word of caution: in preparing a proposal for any work or in writing an initial draft, it is permissible to cite the content of a Dissertation Abstract or a synthesis or abstract of another sort, such as Educational Resources Information Center (ERIC). In *no* final document, should an abstract be used. *Direct reference to the original and complete document is mandatory.*

Rule. In citing an abstract or a microfilmed dissertation, you should add the identifying number. This applies to other such documents, *e.g.*, ERIC microfiche.

In Dwight W. Allen and Frederick J. McDonald's recent study, it is possible to get some understanding of the modeling technique.[1]

---

[1] Frederick J. McDonald and Dwight W. Allen, *Training Effects of Feedback and Modeling Procedures on Teaching Performance*, Palo Alto, California: Stanford Center for Research and Development in Teaching, Stanford University, Technical Report No. 3, U.S. Office of Education — OE-6-10-078, 1967, ERIC ED017-985.

Comment. Our lives, including our footnotes, are increasingly pervaded by numbers.

Bonnie Thoman Engdahl makes it very clear that the colonists, for all of the rigors of their existence, found time to cultivate their gardens.[1]

---

[1] Bonnie Thoman Engdahl, "Paradise in the New World: A Study of the Image of the Garden in the Literature of Colonial America," unpublished dissertation for the Ph.D., Columbia University, 1967, UM #54-6107, 72.

Gerald Monroe's study appears to have dealt with a comparable period, but his population was artists, not actors.[1]

---

[1] Gerald Monroe, "The Artists Union of New York," unpublished dissertation for the Ed.D., New York University, 1971, UM #T6767, in University Microfilms, *Dissertation Abstracts*,[i] Ann Arbor, Michigan: UM, 1972.

---

[i] Again, an "Abstract" would be cited only in a proposal or a preliminary draft, not in a final manuscript.

CHAPTER III
Format

Paper

Paper of good quality should be used for the original typing. Twenty-pound bond, 8½″ x 11″ meets this requirement. Avoid the use of "erasable" paper. It will not take corrections or additions in ink. Xerox copies of your work are acceptable. Whatever you are writing, *be sure to have one copy in your possession at all times.*

Margins

To the extent possible, even margins should be maintained:

- 2 inches on the left (imperative when a manuscript is to be bound)
- 1 inch on the right
- 1 inch at the top and bottom of the page
- 2 inches at the top of the first page of each chapter.

In addition to the pleasant appearance such a format insures, it is necessary to bear in mind the size of the frame used in microfilming. Any page which exceeds these stipulated margins will not fit within the microfilm frame.

No large white space may appear on any page except on the last page of a chapter.

Pagination

The title page and copyright page do not show page numbers. All other pages preliminary to the body of the text should be numbered in lower-case Roman numbers, ½ inch from the bottom of the page. The title page counts as page i. The copyright page (other side of the title page) counts as page ii.

The next page of preliminary matter is numbered page iii. Typing your last name before the number on each page may prevent the misplacing of pages by instructors, committee members, or editors.

The first page of each chapter, though counted in the total enumeration, should not bear a page number.

All pages in the body of the text should have Arabic numerals, ½ inch from the top edge of the page and in the center. Arabic numerals are used not only for the body of the text, but also for all material which might follow the text, *e.g.*, bibliography and appendixes, etc.

Material should be written on one side of the paper only.

If pages are inserted in reports or preliminary drafts of theses after your original pagination, the inserted pages may be indicated by letter transcripts, *e.g.*, 17, 18, 18a, 18b, 19. This practice is *never* permitted in final copies.

All preliminary drafts of dissertation proposals and dissertation chapters should be paginated for easy reference. Pagination may be done in pencil on preliminary drafts to expedite alteration after criticism by sponsors.

Copyright Symbol

In published works, the copyright insignia is placed on the back of the title page. In dissertations, the symbol must be placed on the right-hand page following the title page:

Copyright 1969
by Ulrich Von Hutten

or

© Ulrich Von Hutten 1969

No page number appears on the copyright page.

Spacing

With the exception of indented, single-spaced quotations, or other material indented and single-spaced for emphasis, all of the text should be double-spaced. Footnotes should be single-spaced.

The title of a chapter should be preceded by a chapter heading, *i.e.*, the word "chapter" and the number in Roman numerals. The word "chapter" should be typed in capital letters, one double space below the two-inch margin for the first page of a chapter. The title of the chapter should be typed in capital letters, one double space below the chapter heading. Both

should be centered. The typing which follows, whether straight text or heading, should be three spaces below the chapter title.
Dissertation proposals and term papers do *not* have chapters!

[SAMPLE CHAPTER HEAD]

CHAPTER III
Bibliographic Essay

Heads and Subheads

The head or subhead is followed by a double space. However, between the text and the next head or subhead, there should be three spaces, not two.

Heads and subheads are not mandatory, but in long reports and especially in doctoral dissertations, they are very helpful. An excess of heads and subheads may confuse rather than clarify. The more obfuscatory your writing is, the more you will need heads and subheads to guide the reader through the labyrinth of your words.

Levels of Subheads

A scholarly work frequently requires more than one form of subhead. The more technical or complicated the work, the more levels of subheads may be necessary. The chapter title is centered and in capital letters and subsequent heads relate to it. A "first-order" subhead would, therefore, be a side head. Examples of subheads in declining significance follow.

[FIRST-ORDER SUBHEAD]
Greek Culture of the Golden Age

[SECOND-ORDER SUBHEAD]
Philosophy

[THIRD-ORDER SUBHEAD]
Geographic Differences

[FOURTH-ORDER SUBHEAD]
Climate and Terrain

[FIFTH-ORDER SUBHEAD]
Plato (427-347 B.C.) :

In an actual manuscript, one does not pile subhead upon subhead. Some text should intervene between subheads.

Quotations, Quotation Marks and Ellipses

Rule. Any quotation which is four and one-half or more lines in length *must* be indented and single-spaced. The quotation marks are then deleted. You *may* indent, single-space, and delete quotation marks for quotations of fewer than five lines for purposes of emphasis.

Rule. Quotation marks are placed *outside* periods and commas.

The interesting part of the report dealt with "stereoptic vision."

When Mrs. Malaprop speaks of a "female cemetery," she means a female seminary.

Rule. Quotation marks are placed inside the following punctuation marks: exclamation point, question mark, colon, and semicolon.

Can you imagine his saying, "I'm not concerned"?

There are three foci in Queen's study: "authoritarianism"; "ethnocentrism"; and "totalitarianism."

Exception. When the exclamation point or the question mark is an organic part of the material quoted, the quotation mark is placed outside.

He said, "Woe is me!"

Quotation within a Quotation

Rule. When using a quotation which has a quotation within it, the internal quotation is denoted by a single quotation mark.

"What is our goal? 'The final cause of speech is to get an idea as exactly as possible out of one mind into another. Its formal cause therefore is such choice and disposition of words as will achieve this end most economically.' "[1]

---

[1] Sir Ernest Gowers, *The Complete Plain Words,* London: Her Majesty's Stationery Office, 1954, 1.

Rule. A quotation within an indented, single-spaced quotation, from which quotation marks have been deleted, is placed in double quotation marks.

... one need but to turn to Cervantes: "Do but take care to express yourself in a plain, easy Manner, in well-chosen significant and decent Terms, and to give a harmonious and pleasing Turn to your Periods; study to explain your Thoughts and set them in the truest Light, labouring as much as possible, not to leave them dark or intricate, but clear and intelligible."[2]

---

[2] Sir Ernest Gowers, *The Complete Plain Words*, London: Her Majesty's Stationery Office, 1954, 1, citing Miguel Cervantes, "Preface," *Don Quixote*.

Comment. Take note that in citing a work legitimately considered a classic — such as *Don Quixote* — one merely indicates the source because there are so many editions and translations.

Comment. In citing a work legitimately considered a classic — such as *Don Quixote* — unless you have a particular translation to which you wish the reader to refer, you may indicate the author and title and, if necessary, section. If you do have a particular translation or edition in mind, you must provide the full citation, including all of the detail.

Ellipsis in a Quotation

Rule. When omitting a portion of a quotation, the ellipsis mark is: ... If you omit a very lengthy portion of a quotation — *e.g.*, you wish to cite the beginning of a proposition and the conclusion, but not the explanatory information in between — you use an entire line of spaced periods to indicate the dimension of the elision:

. . . .

Both indices — the three period marks and the entire line — should be typed: period, space, period, space, etc. If the ellipsis mark is at the end of the quotation, the third dot (period) serves as the period of the sentence. It serves as whatever punctuation you have eliminated.

Example

If the original read: "It had a number of parts; some of which were of little use, only one of which interested him, the design for a reclining chair, in genuine leather and teak." and you used only a portion, it might look as follows: "It had a number of parts ... only one of which interested him ... a reclining chair, in genuine leather and teak."

Incomplete Sentence in a Quotation

If the portion you are quoting is not a complete sentence, you *must* place the ellipsis sign before it.

The beggar-like stranger said, ". . . I'm sorry I stopped ye."

If the ellipsis mark had not been used and someone wanted to find that passage, he would be looking for a sentence beginning with "I'm."

Sometimes quotation marks are not included. Follow the format of one of the examples given below.

Not a complete sentence:

. . . but as I strode down the passageway, I saw him and as we passed I saw his [Dente's] lid drop. I hardly knew any of the officers, yet here was one winking at me![3]

Beginning of a sentence, but *not* beginning of a paragraph:

Most of these people had boarded the ship at Sydney. They were, for the most part, Italians, Germans, a few Spanish and Portuguese, some French. They had come to be laborers and to "make their fortunes." They were returning home because, though the money had been good, the working conditions were not . . .[7]

Comment. Take note of the fact that an incompletely quoted sentence must be followed by the . . .

Beginning of a paragraph:

Meantime the chief purser was trying valiantly to find me more suitable quarters. The fact that these were difficult to come by did not seem to daunt him.[5]

Insert in a Quotation

Rule. If you insert a word or words in a quotation to clarify or explain, your insertion must be placed in square brackets: [ ].

The Superior Number

There are various instances in which the superior number is used.

Rule. When using a direct quotation, the superior number appears at the *end of the quotation.*

Kleinman contends that, "The less information available, the simpler is the process of decision-making."[1]

Rule. In narrative discourse, if you paraphrase, the superior number appears at the end.

It has been said that, when there is a paucity of information available, the decision-making process is greatly simplified.[1]

In each of the above instances, the footnote would be the same:

---
[1] Lou Kleinman, "The Decision-Making Process," in *The Letters of Lou Kleinman*, New York: Joni Press, 1972, 2.

Comment. If the above had been a bibliographical reference, it would have been necessary to provide full page information, *i.e.*, instead of just 2, 1–3.

Rule. In narrative discourse, if you mention a series of researchers who elicited the same findings, the superior number is placed at each surname.

This view has been supported in the research of Laurin E. Hyde,[1] Ernest F. Witte,[2] Alice Meeker,[3] and Fred Lewin,[4] all of whom found...

Comment. Each would be a separate and complete footnote.

Rule. If you talk about a concept, a research technique, or an hypothesis tested by a number of people, the superior number appears at the end of the discourse. Then the footnote must incorporate all of the supportive materials.

At least two recent researchers have found that Carl Becker's view of the eighteenth century may be expanded.[1]

---
[1] See: Peter Gay, *The Enlightenment: An Interpretation*, New York: Random House, 1966; and Geoffrey Bruun, *The Benevolent Despots*, New York: The Macmillan Company, 1952.

Citation of Poetry

Great care must be taken to adhere to the laws pertaining to "Fair Use" in citing poetry. If you cite an entire poem, you are, in effect, filching the product of a man's genius. Quoting a line or two of a quatrain is tantamount to stealing half of his wealth. Permission must be obtained to quote more than a "reasonable sample."

Rule. Poetry should be indented and single spaced within stanzas.

So Beautiful You Are Indeed
by Irene Rutherford McLeod

So beautiful you are indeed,
That I am troubled when you come,
And though I crave you for my need,
Your nearness strikes me blind and dumb.

And when you bring your lips to mine,
My spirit trembles and escapes,
And you and I are turned divine,
Bereft of our familiar shapes.

And fearfully we tread cold space,
Naked of flesh and winged with flame,
Until we find us, face to face,
Each calling on the other's name.[1]

---

[1] Irene Rutherford McLeod, "So Beautiful You Are Indeed," in Marguerite Wilkinson, *New Voices*, New York: The Macmillan Company, 1929, 287-288.

Rule. When citing poetry in a footnote or when citing a portion of a poem in the text, slash marks are used to indicate the ends of lines.

> McLeod's simple but telling descriptions linger in one's memory, *e.g.,* "And fearfully we tread cold space, / Naked of flesh and winged with flame, / ..."

Typing Dialogue

Rule. In typing play scripts, it is correct to type the dialogue single-spaced. Double spaces should be used between speeches. Should a character have several paragraphs to say, double spaces should be provided between paragraphs.

Example

John: I am so sorry that I shall be in Los Angeles negotiating a contract while all of you will be having a high old time at dinner and the theatre.

Jason: We're sorry, too.

Helen and Chinita had been looking forward to meeting you so we'll have to arrange another time for getting together when you return.

CHAPTER IV
Documentation through Footnotes

Footnotes are used:

1. to cite the source of a quotation used in the text.
2. to acknowledge the source of an idea stated or the paraphrase of an idea.
3. to bring the weight of authority to support the writer's idea or theory or difference of opinion.
4. to avoid interfering with the reader's thought flow.

Enumeration of Footnotes

In term papers, theses *proposals,* dissertation *proposals,* and drafts of any kind, it is desirable to keep enumeration of footnotes confined to the page. Since drafts are subject to frequent change, sequential enumeration might only lead to extra work and even more confusion. When you have reached some huge number, such as 180, and find that you must insert a footnote between footnote 5 and footnote 6, you must change all of the numbers from six through 180.

In *final copies* of Masters' theses and doctoral dissertations, depending upon what seems most logical and practical, you may continue to enumerate by the page or you may enumerate sequentially within each chapter.

Spacing in Footnotes

The bar dividing the text from the documentation is one double space beneath the last line of the text. The bar is typed with ten connected underscores. The first note is one double space beneath the bar. The number (without a period) should be placed at the left margin and, in this Handbook the number is followed by a space. Some universities prescribe no space after the footnote number.

Example

---

1 Adolphe E. Meyer, *Voltaire: Man of Justice*, New York: Howell, Soskin, 1945, 10-30.
2 Harvey Wish, *Contemporary America*, Second Edition, New York: Harper and Brothers, 1956.

Placement in Footnotes

Rule. Footnotes should be placed where the word itself requires them to be — *i.e.*, at the foot of the page.

Rule. Footnotes have the same status as a sentence; they begin with a capital letter, and end with a period.

Comment. Articles in journals of science, psychology, sociology, etc., frequently have "notes," not "footnotes." Notes appear in numerical sequence at the end of the article. Some books follow this procedure, but the format varies. Some notes appear at the end of each chapter, some at the end of the book.

Dissertations are different. The reader should not be put to the discomfort of bouncing back and forth between the text and the notes. That alone could make him very dizzy and dispose him against the dissertation. Undesirable, to say the least! An additional difficulty is imposed when the footnotes are at the end of the chapter or the end of the book when one is reading microfilm.

Given modern technology and the exponential increase in the use of various microforms, placing notes at the end makes reading anything more and more laborious and might discourage the persons you most want to read your material from doing so. It is much easier to glance down and see the source and the vintage of the material being cited than it is to locate the notes section, no matter where it is placed.

Sample Footnotes

Footnote for an Article

Randall states that there are things to examine about Plato which are not to be found in the *Dialogues*.[1]

---

1 John Herman Randall, Jr., "Plato As the Philosopher of the Artistic Experience," *The American Scholar*, Summer, 1968, 37:3, 2.

Sequence in Footnote for an Article. The footnote, as a general rule, follows the form which would be required by the publisher or copyright holder in granting permission for the citation of the material. The sequence follows: 1) author's name, *first name first*; 2) title of the article in quotation marks; 3) title of the journal in italics (underscored); 4) date of the issue: if a *weekly*, month, day, year; if a *biweekly*, month, year; if a *quarterly*, season, year; and if an *annual*, year; 5) volume number, which should be precisely what is used on the journal, *i.e.*, if Arabic, then Arabic, if Roman, then Roman; 6) issue number; and 7) page or pages. Look back at the example. Note that all of the punctuation is commas, until the volume number and issue number, which are separated by a colon, *i.e.*, 37:3. The issue number is separated from the page by a comma again, *i.e.*, 37:3, 2. Other page citations might be 37:3, 2-12; 37:3, 2,7 and 10; 37:3, 22 *et passim;* or 37:3, *passim*.[i]

Rule. Neither volume nor issue numbers are required for a daily or weekly, only the complete date, *e.g.*, January 22, 1972, and page or pages.

Footnote for a Book

[IN THE TEXT]

The Eskimo male does get involved in violent physical aggression and, "surprisingly enough, the apparent cause in his sexually lax society is adultery."[1]

[FOOTNOTE]

[1] Peter Farb, *Man's Rise to Civilization, As Shown by the Indians of North America from Primeval Times to the Coming of the Industrial State* hereinafter *Man's Rise to Civilization*, New York: E.P. Dutton and Co., Inc., 1968, 43.

Comment. If you are going to make much use of a book with a title of that dimension, you should devise a shortened title. See footnote example above.

Sequence in Footnote for a Book. The sequence follows: 1) author's name, *first name first*; 2) title of the book, in italics (underscored); 3) place of publication; 4) publisher; 5) year of publication; and 6) page or pages.

Footnote for a Chapter in a Book or an Essay in a Collection of Essays

This form is identical with the form for a footnote for an article. The chapter title or essay title replaces the title for an article; the book title replaces the journal. As always, there are exceptions. Collected essays or an anthology usually have an author or authors or an editor or editors. Such books frequently have a foreword by yet another person. The examples which follow go from the most simple to the most complex.

[i] See Chapter IX, "Foreign Words and Abbreviations," 90–91.

[1] W. W. Charters, Jr. and N. L. Gage, eds., *Readings in the Social Psychology of Education*, Boston: Allyn and Bacon, 1963.

[2] W. W. Charters, Jr. and N. L. Gage, eds., *Readings in the Social Psychology of Education*, Boston: Allyn and Bacon, 1963, "Introduction," xv.

[3] Goodwin Watson, "Foreword," in W. W. Charters, Jr. and N. L. Gage, eds., *Readings in the Social Psychology of Education*, Boston: Allyn and Bacon, 1963, vii.

[4] Kurt Lewin, *Resolving Social Conflict*, New York: Harper & Row, Publishers, 1948, 67, cited by Dorwin Cartwright, "Achieving Change in People: Some Applications of Group Dynamics Theory," in W. W. Charters, Jr. and N. L. Gage, eds., *Readings in the Social Psychology of Education*, Boston: Allyn and Bacon, 1963, 111.

Comment. Each of the foregoing footnotes is to be looked upon as a *first* citation. There are many things to be observed. The publisher's name must be copied exactly as it appears in the book, no matter how lengthy, *e.g.*, The McFine Book Company, Inc. The "Foreword,"[i] "Preface" or "Introduction" should be specified. Suppose you found a quotation from Lewin in Cartwright. Don't document the Lewin material alone with no reference to Cartwright. However, if the Lewin quotation was of such importance, it might have been better to go back to the original. This is recommended not only to shorten the footnote, but also to insure that Cartwright quoted accurately.

The author of the material being quoted takes precedence over the editors, as in the Watson footnote; the author of the material being quoted takes precedence over the author of the essay, and the author of the essay takes precedence over the editors. Every word in a title, except articles and prepositions, should have an initial capital.

When you are using several articles or essays or chapters from a compilation or anthology, you need give complete information in only the first citation.

Examples

[1] George M. Trevelyan, "Some Points of Contrast between Medieval and Modern Society," in Karl de Schweinitz, Jr. and Kenneth W. Thompson, with the collaboration of Paul K. Hatt, *Man and Modern Society, Conflict and Choice in the Industrial Era*, New York: Henry Holt and Co., 1953, 28.

[2] Max Weber, "On Bureaucracy," in de Schweinitz and Thompson, 502.

[3] Karl de Schweinitz, Jr., "Tension among Nations," in de Schweinitz and Thompson, 705.

[4] Karl de Schweinitz, Jr. and Kenneth W. Thompson, "Preface," in de Schweinitz and Thompson, vii.

[i] "Foreword" is correct. "Forward" is not!

Documenting the Classics

A special form is used in citing and documenting a classical work. If you are going to refer to a particular edition throughout your paper, provide a footnote.

Examples

1 All references to the Bible throughout this MS. will be to *The Holy Bible*, Revised Standard Version, New York: Thomas and Sons, 1953.

2 Micah, VI:3.

Comment. Note that, since you have established the edition, you need cite only the book, the chapter, and the verse or verses. The title of the book is unalloyed, *i.e.*, not in italics, not in quotation marks. The title is followed by a comma, the chapter is in Roman numbers, followed by a colon, followed by the Arabic number or numbers for the verse or verses.

In citing other classical works, *i.e.*, a play by Shakespeare[i] or a work by Dante — if you use a particular edition, provide a footnote comparable to the one provided for the Bible.

Examples

1 All references to *The Divine Comedy* will be to Dante Alighieri, The Florentine, *The Divine Comedy*, The Penguin Classics, 3 vols., Middlesex, England: Penguin Books, *The Divine Comedy*, Cantica I, *Hell (L'Inferno)*, trans. by Dorothy L. Sayers, 1972; *The Divine Comedy*, Cantica II, *Purgatory (Il Purgatorio)*, trans. by Dorothy L. Sayers, 1967; and *The Divine Comedy*, Cantica III, *Paradise (Il Paradiso)*, trans. by Dorothy L. Sayers and Barbara Reynolds, 1967.

2 *The Divine Comedy*, I, Canto XX, Circle VIII, iv:82-87; II, Canto XIV, Cornice II, 37-39; and III, Canto XX, 37-42.

Comment. If you are going to deal only with Dante (and it is obvious that he is a rather special and complicated case), you may omit his name after the first footnote in which you have supplied the complete data.

In documenting classical plays — such as those of Aeschylus, Sophocles, Euripedes, Aristophanes, or Plautus — or other classical works,[ii] *e.g.*, works by Aristotle, Plato, Moses Maimonides, John Locke — the titles *are* in italics. If the work being documented is a play, part of which is being cited, the title is followed by a comma, the act is in Roman numbers, followed by a colon, the scene is in lower-case Roman numbers, followed by a comma, and the line or lines are in Arabic numbers.[iii]

---

[i] See Chapter VII, "The Term Paper," 69.

[ii] See Chapter III, "Format," 25.

[iii] See Chapter VIII, "The Method," 85, footnote ii.

Example

[1] *Macbeth,* II:ii, 36-41.

If the work being documented is not a play, the form is dictated by the structure used by the original author or translator. The most prevalent form would present the title in italics, followed by a comma, followed by the major section in Roman numbers, followed by a colon, followed by the subsection in lower-case Roman numbers, followed by a comma, and the line or lines in Arabic numbers, followed by a period. When referring to a line or lines in the text, the abbreviation is l. or ll.[i] The examples which follow indicate the great structural variety to be found in classical works.

Examples

[1] Aristotle, *On Generation and Corruption,* I:viii, 326^a, 1-10.

[2] Plato, *Laws,* V, 727-728^{b-e}.

[3] Moses Maimonides [Moses ben Maimon], *The Guide of the Perplexed,* translated with an introduction and notes by Shlomo Pines, with an introductory essay by Leo Strauss, Chicago: The University of Chicago Press, 1964, I:49, 26^a-56^b.

[4] John Locke, *An Essay concerning Human Understanding,* abridged and edited by A. S. Pringle-Pattison, Oxford: At the Clarendon Press, 1950.

[5] Locke, "Of Retention," II:x, 1-5.

Footnote for a Dissertation, Master's Thesis, Mimeographed Paper

Rule. Titles of dissertations, Masters' theses, and mimeographed papers are *not* italicized — *i.e.,* they are *not* underscored in typescript.

Examples

[DOCTORAL DISSERTATION]

[1] Albert Hofstadter, "Locke and Skepticism," unpublished dissertation for the Ph.D., Ohio State University, 1912.

[MASTER'S THESIS]

[6] Emma A. Cahill, "The Comparative View of Locke and Rousseau on History," unpublished A.M. thesis, New York University, 1936.

[MIMEOGRAPHED REPORT]

[3] Christopher Dock, "The Orderly School," A Report to the Board of Advisors of the Commonwealth of Pennsylvania, 1968, mimeographed.

---

[i] See Appendix A, "Singular and Plural Forms," 96-97.

Legal Documentation

Although great emphasis has been and will be placed on simplicity, economy and precision throughout this book, in no other writing is it more important than in matters of law. As in every profession, the law has a special language; it also has its own form of documentation. If you are going to deal with legal citations extensively, you should make a careful study of the entire panoply of rules and regulations for legal writing. Your local Association of the Bar and the librarian of a law school should be able to direct you to good sources.[i]

As a general procedure, all legal citations should follow the exact way in which the case is cited.

Example

[1] Jones v. Lucas, 432 Pa. 296, 32 B.3rd 623 (1951).

That is a relatively simple citation, but it clearly indicates the form such footnotes take. Henry Weihofen cites a more complex footnote.

Example

[6] Knott v. Rawlings, 250 Iowa 892, 96 N.W. 2nd 900 (1959). See also Application of Smith, 351 P.2d 1076 (OKL.CR.1960), interpreting a statutory definition of rape "by a male over eighteen years of age."[ii]

Custom varies sharply in the use of italics in citing cases. However, unlike the cases cited above, customarily legal citations use the abbreviation v. for versus, not italicized, and italicize the names of the adversaries.

Example

[1] *Edmunds* v. *Bureau of Revenue of the State of New Mexico*, 330 P. (2d) 131 (N.M.).

It is unlikely that in your lifetime — a long one it is hoped — or mine, probably much shorter, any drastic change will take place in the cluttered and obscure forms which have accrued about the law for thousands of years. Therefore, it is obligatory, if you are using legal citations, that you follow custom.

---

[i] An excellent book on legal writing and documentation is: Henry Weihofen, *Legal Writing Style*, 2nd ed., St. Paul, Minn.: West Publishing Co., 1980.

[ii] Weihofen, 10.

Documentation for Paraphrase

Rule. If you attribute ideas to someone else, paraphrase someone else's words, or use someone else's view of something, give him credit!

Examples

John Dewey believed that it was necessary to improve a person's view of the value of his own work.[1]

---

[1] John Dewey, *Democracy and Education*, New York: The Macmillan Company, 1916, 98.

It is important to engage a person's interest in his work.[2]

---

[2] John Dewey, *Democracy and Education*, New York: The Macmillan Company, 1916, 98.

The notion that only a professional position may be viewed as a vocation is deleterious to a democratic society.[3]

---

[3] John Dewey, *Democracy and Education*, New York: The Macmillan Company, 1916, 98.

An even more complex form of citation in this category follows:

John Dewey expounds upon the notion of the value of vocation.[4] One cannot help wondering whether he was familiar with an earlier, more persuasive argument in the same vein.[5]

---

[4] John Dewey, *Democracy and Education*, New York: The Macmillan Company, 1916, 98, *et passim.*

[5] See the concept of *Beruf*, Max Weber, *The Protestant Ethic and the Spirit of Capitalism*, New York: Charles Scribner's Sons, 1956, 79-92.

Place of Publication

Comment. In citing the place of publication, if the title page uses "New York, N.Y.," you must so cite it. If it uses "Boston" only, you do not supply "Mass." If the title page cites a variety of places of publication, *e.g.*, "New York, London and Toronto," you cite only "New York."

Documenting within a Chapter

Rule. In the writing of a dissertation, to facilitate reference by the reader, *complete citations should be given within each chapter, when a book, article, anthology, etc. is documented.* In other words, if a reference is repeated in another chapter of the dissertation, the complete citation must be given again.

Rule. When writing a term paper, unlike a document with several chapters, it is *not* necessary to repeat the total information once a full citation has been given for a book, article, anthology, etc.

Repeated Citations of the Same Work

Rule. Once a work has been completely documented, either in a term paper or in a chapter, the following examples will indicate the way in which additional documentation should be done.

Examples

[FIRST FOOTNOTE]

1 John Dewey, *Democracy and Education*, New York: The Macmillan Company, 1916, 98.

[SECOND FOOTNOTE]

2 *Ibid.*

Comment. If you are using not only *Democracy and Education*, but also one or more other works by Dewey, the footnotes should read:

2 Dewey, *Art as Experience*, 22.

3 Dewey, *Democracy and Education*, 102.

Multiple Authors or Editors

Rule. When several authors or editors are involved in one footnote, use the following format.

Example

[FIRST FOOTNOTE]

1 Jerome S. Bruner, Jacqueline J. Goodnow and George A. Austin, *A Study of Thinking*, New York: Science Editions, Inc., 1962, 1.

[SECOND FOOTNOTE]

8 Bruner, et al., 2.

Organization As Author

Rule. When an organization or committee has produced the book or monograph, and no author or editor is given, the organization or committee becomes the author.

Example

1 American Historical Association, *Guides for the Teaching of History*, Washington, D.C.: The Association, 1962.

Comment. If you are going to use a number of publications in which the American Historical Association is to be cited as the author, it would be well to follow the first citation with:

, hereinafter AHA,

Note that "The Association," a truncated version of the entire name, is cited as the publisher.

Missing Information

Occasionally a pamphlet or brochure seems to have sprung from a cloud, lacking author, editor, publisher, and date. It may also be unpaginated. You cannot be expected to cite more than is available, but you should have exhausted every means to provide as much data as possible. If you have failed on all scores, the citation is simple:

1 *Rights for All*, no other information available, unpaginated.

If only the publisher and his geographic location are missing, the citation would be:

1 *Rights for All*, n.p.:n.n.,[i] 1984, 26.

If the publisher and his geographic location were available, but not the date, the citation would read:

1 *Rights for All*, New York: Underground Press, n.d.,[i] 86.

If all the information is available, but the work is unpaginated, the citation would be:

1 *Rights for All*, New York: Underground Press, 1971, unpaginated.

---

[i] See Chapter IX, 89-91.

Ibid.

Rule. When referring to precisely the same work cited immediately above, use *Ibid.* You may carry *Ibid.* over from one page to another.

Examples

8 Edward T. Hall, *The Silent Language*, Greenwich, Conn.: A Fawcett Premier Book, 1959.

9 *Ibid.*, 39.

10 *Ibid.*

11 *Ibid.*, 22.

Comment. Note that the second line of a footnote goes directly to the left margin. Note, too, that *Ibid.* has an initial capital, since it is the first word in the footnote. It is an abbreviation and, therefore, is followed only by a period when it stands alone; by a period and a comma when it is followed by a page number.

Rule. You may *not* use *Ibid.* after a complex citation.

Example

22 Roger W. Sperry, "Physiological Plasticity and Brain Circuit Theory," in H.F. Harlow and C.N. Woolsey, eds., *New Theories in Science*, Madison: University of Wisconsin Press, 1958, 401-424.

Comment. If you used *Ibid.*, to what would you be ibiding?

The way you would handle the next citation would depend on which portion of the first citation you wished to refer to.

Examples

23 Sperry, 423.

23 Harlow and Woolsey, eds., 426.

Since you may be copying and will be reading the footnotes of other people, you should know the meaning of all the terms which you will encounter.[1] You will be using *only* the terms cited in this book.

---

[1] See Chapter IX, "Foreign Words and Abbreviations," 89-91.

Personal Communication: Interview, Letter, Telephone Call

If you get information or conduct an interview by telephone, you must provide precise data about the circumstances.

Examples

Dr. Nathaniel Uhr distinctly remembered that "Pop" Hart had spent at least a year painting in Mexico.[1]

---

[1] Telephone interview with Nathaniel Uhr, M.D., Chief of Medicine, The Menninger Foundation, Topeka, Kansas, June 10, 1969.

If the interview had been in person, the following would have been the citation:

---

[2] Personal interview with Nathaniel Uhr, M.D., Chief of Medicine, The Menninger Foundation, Topeka, Kansas, June 10, 1969.

If the information had been communicated in a letter, the following would have been the citation:

---

[3] Letter from Nathaniel Uhr, M.D., Chief of Medicine, The Menninger Foundation, Topeka, Kansas, June 10, 1969, 3.

Comment. If the letter has more than one page, then the page containing the material you are using must be cited. When entering letters in your bibliography, however, you must provide the precise number of pages in each letter. In the above case, it might be 1-3.

Lecture Notes

If you use information obtained at a public lecture or as part of a class lecture, you must provide precise documentation.

Examples

---

[1] John P. Spiegel, M.D., lecture delivered for the course "Contemporary Problems in Education: Interdisciplinary Analysis," School of Education, New York University, New York, N.Y., October 21, 1969.

---

[2] John P. Spiegel, M.D., address delivered to the American Orthopsychiatric Association, Waldorf-Astoria Hotel, New York, N.Y., February 6, 1968.

Comment. 1. If either address had had a title, it should have been included immediately after the speaker's name and title, in quotation marks.
2. When you quote from a lecture in a term paper, a Master's thesis, or a doctoral dissertation, you should submit the material, exactly as you plan to use it, to the author for approval. This applies as well to material derived from telephone conversations or letters.

Newspaper Articles

When citing newspaper articles, include author (if given), title of article, name of publication, date of publication, and page number.

Examples

[ARTICLE WITH A BYLINE]

[1] David Gates, "Ecological Principles and the Environment," *The New York Times*, April 28, 1971, 22.

[STAFF WRITER]

[1] "Student Unrest," *The New York Times*, April 7, 1971, 36.

[SUNDAY — *The New York Times*]

[1] Michael Drosnin, "Ripping Off, The New Life Style," *The New York Times Magazine*, August 8, 1971, 13.

[2] Patricia Hubbell, "A Place for Earthlings to Wander Among Some Rocks," *The New York Times*, August 8, 1971, D 25.

Volumes, Editions, Revisions

As with all books, the first time you refer to a work with more than one volume, complete citation should be made. This applies as well to revisions of books and editions.

Examples

[1] Dumas Malone and Basil Rauch, *Empire for Liberty*, The Genesis and Growth of the United States of America, 2 vols., New York: Appleton-Century-Crofts, Inc., 1960, II, 596.

Comment. Note that the citation of the precise volume from which material has been quoted appears immediately before the page. It could have been "I, 362." In all subsequent citations from that work, a greatly abbreviated footnote would be acceptable. If no other work by precisely the same authors has been or will be used in the manuscript, all that would be needed follows.

---

2 Malone and Rauch, II, 636.

---

1 Adolphe E. Meyer, *An Educational History of the American People*, Revised Edition, New York: McGraw-Hill Book Co., Inc., 1966.

---

2 Meyer, 102.

Books by One Author, Revised by Another

A citation from a book by one author, but revised or edited by another author or authors, requires inclusion of both authors, with the original author taking precedence. If the work is multivolumed, so specify. Once all that information has been given in the first citation, subsequent documentation need provide only the necessary data.

Examples

[FIRST CITATION]

---

1 Hastings Rashdall, *The Universities of Europe in the Middle Ages*, 1895, 3 vols., F. M. Powicke and A. B. Emden, eds., Oxford: At the Clarendon Press, 1936, I, 210.

[SUBSEQUENT CITATIONS]

---

5 Rashdall, III, 86.

Citation of Reissued Books

To protect your own reputation for intelligence and integrity, it is necessary to keep the reader informed about the vintage of a book. Sometimes, because of copyright provisions, it is necessary to cite the original publisher, too.

Example

---

1 Johan Huizinga, *Homo Ludens*, Great Britain: Routledge and Kegan Paul Ltd., 1949, Paladin, 1971.

2 Hastings Rashdall, *The Universities of Europe in the Middle Ages*, 1895, 3 vols., F. M. Powicke and A. B. Emden, eds., Oxford: At the Clarendon Press, 1936, II, 52.

Documentation through Footnotes: A Summary

For an Article
John Herman Randall, Jr., "Plato As the Philosopher of the Artistic Experience," *The American Scholar*, Summer, 1968, 37:3,2.

For a Book
John Dewey, *Art as Experience*, New York: Minton, Balch and Co., 1934.

For a Chapter in a Book or an Essay in a Collection of Essays
Celestine Fulchon, "Handling the Depressed Adolescent," in W.W. Charters, Jr. and N.L. Gage, eds. *Readings in the Social Psychology of Education*, Boston: Allyn and Bacon, 1963, 98–111.

For a Classic
Dante Alighieri, The Florentine, *The Divine Comedy*, The Penguin Classics, 3 vols., Middlesex, England: Penguin Books, trans. by Dorothy L. Sayers, 1972, I, Canto XX, Circle VIII, iv:82–87.

For a Play
William Shakespeare, *Macbeth*, II;ii,36–41.

For a Dissertation, Master's Thesis, Mimeographed Paper
Albert Hofstadter, "Locke and Skepticism," unpublished dissertation for the Ph.D., Ohio State University, 1912.

For a Book with no Author's Name
Webster's Biographical Dictionary, Springfield, Mass.: G.&C. Merriam Co., 1968, 224.

For an Encyclopedia Article
Parke Cummings, "Sports, Athletic," *Encyclopedia Americana*, vols. 30, New York: Americana Corporation, 1971, XXV, 434d–443.

For an Interview
Interview with Nathaniel Uhr, M.D., Chief of Medicine, The Menninger Foundation, Topeka, Kansas, June 10, 1969.

For an Unsigned Pamphlet
Department of Agriculture of the United States, *Soil Erosion and Flood Control*, Washington, D.C.: U.S. Government Printing Office, 1972, 31.

For an Anthology
Peter Viereck, "Kilroy," in *Modern American and British Poetry*, ed. by Louis Untermeyer, New York: Harcourt Brace & World, Inc., 1967, 374.

For a Lecture
John P. Spiegel, M.D., lecture delivered for the course "Contemporary Problems in Education: Interdisciplinary Analysis," School of Education, New York University, New York, N.Y., October 21, 1969.

CHAPTER V
Bibliography

The bibliography of a scholarly paper lists the sources used by the writer of the paper. The bibliography does not include every source that the writer has examined. It should, however, include every source that the writer has found pertinent to what he is trying to express in his paper.

Bibliographic Classification

There are many ways in which a bibliography may be divided. A physical classification is commonly used: Books, Journals, Brochures, Monographs, Newspapers, Manuscripts. Another classification method is that of source status: Primary Sources, Secondary Sources.

Rule. Logic and practicality should guide your construction of your bibliography, as well as the decision to present it in sections or as a totality.

Rule. Illustrations, *e.g.*, photographs of art works, recordings, *e.g.*, tapes, cassettes, or phonograph records, and other such artifacts should be listed in separate sections. Separate sections should be provided, too, for letters and interviews.

Comment. Most dissertations will, in themselves, fall into logical sections. In the same way, the bibliographies will fall into logical sections.

For example, a dissertation dealing with both theology and history would have sections on each of those categories. It is clear that division by subject is both more logical and more practical than division by form of publication.

Rule. In cases where actual manuscripts or holographs (documents wholly written by hand) are a basic part of the resources used in a dissertation, they should be listed separately from printed materials.

Spacing and Indenting the Bibliography

Rule. The first line of a bibliography entry should begin at the left margin. Subsequent lines should be indented six to ten spaces. Bibliographic entries are typed single-space with a double space between the entries.

Bibliographic Entries

Bibliographic entries are listed alphabetically by author. In the absence of an author *per se,* an organization or governmental department may become the author of record. In the absence of author, organization, or governmental department, the entry is alphabetical by title.

Examples

Huxley, Thomas H. *Man's Place in Nature.* 1863. With introduction by Ashley Montagu. Ann Arbor, Michigan: The University of Michigan Press, 1959.
U.S. Department of Health, Education and Welfare, "Office of Education, Copyright Guidelines," OE 11030. Washington, D.C.: U.S. Government Printing Office, 1969, 22–36.
Vernon Associates. *The Death of the World.* New York: Ecology Press, 1971.
Wilderness Society. *The Rebirth of the World.* New York: The Society, 1982.
Workshop in Cross-Cultural Education Summary Reports and Project Evaluation. New York: Bilingual Press, 1983.

If you decide to have separate sections within your bibliography, the entries within each section should appear in alphabetical order. Occasionally bibliographies are divided according to the content of each chapter. This should be done only if there is a clearly defined, separate subject for each chapter.

Sequence of Bibliographic Entry of a Book

The sequence for each bibliographic entry of a book is: 1) author's name (or names), *last name first*; 2) title of published book in italics (underscored); 3) place of publication; 4) name of publisher in full detail; 5) year of publication.

Examples

Fine, Paul. *The International Commodities Market.* Nanuet, New York: The Pauline Press, 1973.
Syriotis, Nicholas and Syriotis, Ivy. *Mail Order Marketing.* Bennington, Vermont: The Forman Press, 1972.

Comment. Note that the author's name (or names) is followed by a period, as is the title of the book; the place of publication is followed by a colon; the publisher's name is followed by a comma; and the date of publication is followed by a period.

Sequence of Bibliographic Entry of Essay, Article, Etc.

The sequence for a bibliographic entry of an essay, an article in a newspaper, journal or magazine, or a chapter, etc., is: 1) author's name (or names), *last name first*; 2) title of article, essay, etc., in quotation marks; 3) an editor or editors are cited next; 4) title of the actual published work in italics (underscored); 5) if a chapter in a book, place of publication, name of publisher in full, year of publication, complete information on pages; 6) if an article or essay in a journal, magazine, etc., complete date;[i] 7) volume number and issue number; 8) pages.

Examples

Rosenthal, Steven, "Teaching the Literature of the Bible," in Lila Rosenblum, ed., *The Creative English Teacher,* New York: The Blustain Press, 1963, 32-46.
Silverblank, Stanley, "The Compleat Golfer," *The Sportsman,* January, 1973, VII:3, 23-50.

Comment. Note that the author's name is followed by a comma and that commas prevail with the exceptions of the colon between volume number and issue number and of the closing period.

Rule. When citing articles from journals in which the pagination may not be sequential, you must supply all of the pages.

Example

Bierman, Frederick, "The New Doctor," *The Scalpel,* March, 1974, X:3, 22-23, 35, 59-60.

---

[i] See Chapter IV, "Footnote for an Article," 31.

Comment. You do *not* have to supply the total number of pages for books.

Sequence of Bibliographic Entry of More Than One Book by the Same Author

If you are citing more than one book by the same author, you should list them alphabetically by *title*. There is a device for use in bibliographies *only* to avoid repeating the author's name. It *may not* be used in documenting (footnoting) even when citing books by the same author sequentially.

Example

Dewey, John. *Art As Experience.* New York: The John Day Company, 1932.
_____. *Democracy and Education.* New York: The Macmillan Company, 1916.

Comment. The bar used instead of the author's name is made of ten strokes of the underscore key, beginning at the initial capital of the author's surname, and is followed by a period.

Citing from a Compilation or Anthology

If you have cited an article or articles from a compilation or anthology, you should cite each article by author separately, as well as the compilation. The citation of the compilation is the most extensive one. If the first entry is an article or chapter within the compilation, provide complete data. The entry for the compilation itself should have complete data. Any other portion of the compilation requires only a partial entry.

Example

Blauner, Robert, "Internal Colonialism and Ghetto Revolt," in James A. Geschwender, ed. *The Black Revolt.* Englewood Cliffs, New Jersey: Prentice-Hall, Inc., 1971, 233–250.
Franklin, Raymond S. "The Political Economy of Black Power," in James A. Geschwender, ed. *The Black Revolt.* 216-233.
Geschwender, James A., ed. *The Black Revolt.* Englewood Cliffs, New Jersey: Prentice-Hall, 1971.

Citing Multiple Authors

When citing a work with multiple authors, provide precise detail on each author.

Example

Smiley, Marjorie B. and Diekhoff, John S. *Prologue to Teaching.* New York: Oxford University Press, 1959.

No matter how great the number of authors, give each one his full identification.

Comment. Every item you have used in a footnote should appear in the bibliography. The tendency to puff and pad bibliographies is to be deplored. Only if you can, in good conscience, support the inclusion of an item not actually used and cited in the text should you include it in the bibliography.

Sample Bibliography

The following is a truncated version of a bibliography. Assume that it would have begun with the two-inch margin at the top required for a chapter. It exemplifies that form of bibliography in which the several divisions were a product of the topics contained in the dissertation. Note that the sections were not determined by the type of publication, *i.e.*, published books, journals, etc.

Bibliography

Manuscripts
Banks, Sir John, Letter from Sir John Banks to John Locke, B.L.[i] MSS. Locke, c.3, f.88, 1677.
Churchill, Awnsham, Letter from Awnsham Churchill to John Locke, 17 November, 1703, B.L. MSS. Locke, c.5, f.202.
Locke, John, Annotated holograph of William Penn's The First Frame of Government and Pensilvania Laws, B.L. MSS. Locke, f.9, 33-41.
—————. Fragment, John Locke to Edward Clarke (?), B.L. MSS. Locke, c.11, f.197.

The Works of John Locke[ii]
Locke, John. Aesop's Fables, in English and Latin, Interlineary, for the Benefit of those who Not having a Master, Would Learn Either of these Tongues. With Sculptures. London: Printed for A. and J. Churchill at the Black Swan in Pater-noster-row, 1703. B.L. 2905, e.2.
—————. An Essay Concerning Human Understanding. Abridged and Edited by A.S. Pringle-Pattison. First Edition, 1924. Oxford: At the Clarendon Press, 1950.
Works on or Pertaining to John Locke

---

[i] An abbreviation section would have been provided informing the reader, long before the bibliography, that B.L. was to mean Bodleian Library. See: Chapter II, "Abbreviations," 18-19, and Chapter IX, "Foreign Words and Abbreviations," 92.

[ii] **Note that the title page must be cited exactly.**

Aaron, Richard I. John Locke. Second Edition. Oxford: At the Clarendon Press, 1955.
Arnstaedt, Dr. F.A. François Rabelais und sein Traité d'Education mit besonderer Berücksichtigung der pädagogischen Grundsatze Montaigne's, Locke's und Rousseau's. Leipsig, 1872.[i]
Gibb, Jocelyn, "Introduction," to John Locke. An Early Draft of Locke's Essay, Together with Excerpts from His Journals. R.I. Aaron and Jocelyn Gibbs, eds. Oxford: At the Clarendon Press, 1936.
Johnson, Laura Elizabeth, "John Locke As a Religious Educator," unpublished thesis for the A.M., New York University, 1931.
McNeil, John T. D.D., "The Dissenting Tradition," in Frederick Ernest Johnson, ed., Institute of Religious and Sociological Studies of the Jewish Theological Seminary. New York and London: Harper and Brothers, 1948, 20-50.
Whitehead, Alfred North. Science and the Modern World. 1925. New York: The Macmillan Company, Pelican-Mentor Books, 1948.
Wishy, Bernard, "John Locke and the Spirit of '76," Political Science Quarterly, September, 1958, LXXIII:3, 413, 417-420.

Pennsylvania and Penn

Barker, Joseph A. The Life of William Penn, The Celebrated Quaker and Founder of Pennsylvania. London: Sold by J. Chapman, 121 Newgate Street, Wortley, near Leeds, Printed and Sold by Joseph Barker, 1847.
Cubberly, Elwood P. and Elliott, Edward G. State and County School Administration. Vol. II "Source Book." Vol. I was never published.[ii] New York: The Macmillan Company, 1927.
Douglas, Paul H. American Apprenticeship and Industrial Education. Studies in History, Economics and Public Law. Edited by the Faculty of Political Science of Columbia University. New York: Columbia University Press, 1921. XCV:2. Whole Number. Published also as a dissertation for the degree of doctor of philosophy, Columbia University, 1921.[iii]
Scott, Walter, "Marmion," in The Poetical Works of Sir Walter Scott. New York: D. Appleton & Co., 92 and 94 Grand Street, 1868.

The Sects and the Schoolmasters

Doll, Eugene E. The Ephrata Cloister, An Introduction. Ephrata, Pennsylvania: Ephrata Cloister Associates, Inc., 1958.

---

[i] No amount of exploration could unearth a publisher for this work; only place of publication and year could be supplied.

[ii] This is one of the weirder entries, but it is the kind of information you must track down and supply.

[iii] Note the complexities and detail for this one.

Dunlap, William C. Quaker Education in Baltimore and Virginia Yearly Meetings, with an account of Certain Meetings of Delaware and the Eastern Shore affiliated with Philadelphia; based on the manuscript sources. Philadelphia: Published by the Author, 1936.
Fox, George. Journal. Two Vols. Edited from the MSS. by Norman Penney, with an introduction by T. Edmund Harvey. London: Cambridge University Press, 1911.
Reformed Church Publication Board. Minutes and Letters of the Coetus of the German Reformed Congregation in Pennsylvania 1747-1792, Together with Three Preliminary Reports of Reverend John Philip Boehm, 1734-1744. Research and Translation by Rev. J.I. Good, D.D. and Rev. Prof. Wm. J. Hinke, in America and Holland. Philadelphia: The Board, 1903.
Sachse, Julius Friedrich, "Benjamin Furly, 'An English Merchant at Rotterdam,' Who Promoted the First Emigration to America," The Pennsylvania Magazine of History and Biography, October, 1895, 19:3, 277-306.

James Logan, Benjamin Franklin, William Smith, and the Academy
Curti, Merle. The Social Ideas of American Educators. New York: Charles Scribner's Sons, 1935.
Fäy, Bernard. Franklin, the Apostle of Modern Times. Boston: Little, Brown and Company, 1929.
Smith, William, D.D., Provost of the Said College and Academy. Account of the College, Academy and Charitable School of Philadelphia in Pennsylvania, 1756. With a Commentary and Notes by Thomas Woody, Ph.D., Edited by Thomas R. Adams. Philadelphia: University of Pennsylvania Library, 1951.

Letters to the Writer
Bill, E.G.W., Librarian, Lambeth Palace Library, London, 29 January 1959, 1-3; London, 2 February 1963, 1-2.
de Beer, Esmond S., London, 7 February 1959, 1-2; Oxford, 10 June 1959, 1-4; Raasay, 18 August 1960, 1-3; London, 3 February 1962, 1-4; London, Section I, 5 April 1962, 1-5, London, Section II, 6 April 1962, 1-4.

General References
Gottschalk, Louis. Understanding History. New York: Alfred A. Knopf, 1956.
Nevins, Allan. The Gateway to History, New York: Doubleday & Company, Inc., 1963.

Special Bibliographic Lists

In a dissertation on music, one might have a separate list of manuscripts and recordings. If several recording companies have produced a number of recordings, subheadings by company might be useful. Lists of recordings should include: composer; title of composition; recording artists; type of recording, *e.g.*, monaural, stereo, 33⅓ or 45 rpm, shellac, vinyl, cassette, tape; number; recording company; date.

When a considerable number of articles has been used from one newspaper, one might cite the paper as author and then list all of the articles, by specific author, if a by-line is present, or by title, with dates and pages.

In a historical study, one might wish to list the materials chronologically.

An art paper or dissertation would require lists of illustrations or photographs. A paper with extensive charts, tables, and graphs would provide lists of these in the table of contents.[1] Some manuscripts list all of these both in the table of contents and the bibliography. Abide by what is required by your school or editor.

---

[1] See Chapter X, "Table of Contents," 94–95.

CHAPTER VI
Tables, Figures, Charts, Graphs, Illustrations

Appropriate Use

Another facet of the difficulty which pervades scholarly research and documentation, aside from the mode of presentation, is the obsession with "looking scientific." This is frequently evidenced in exposition which befuddles rather than clarifies. Even more frequently, "scientific" is equated with numbers. The language of statistics and the visual expression of them, in tables, charts, graphs, *et al.*, are injected with little or no regard to their appropriateness or the internal consistency of their use. All of this, unfortunately, produces pseudoscientific—not intrinsically scientific—material.

One evidence of this tendency is the way in which tables and figures are numbered. Imitation has been said to be the highest form of flattery but, when inappropriate, it labels the imitator either an incompetent, or worse, a fool. In truly scientific and mathematic term papers, theses, or dissertations, it is sometimes necessary to use a notation system which sets the relationship between a central theme and its corollary data. For example, a significant theorem may be the focus of discussion and a series of proofs thereof are to be explicated. The obvious procedure, for ease of reference, is:

>   Theorem 1.
>   Proof 1.1
>   Proof 1.2
>   Proof 1.3
>
>   *or*
>
>   Formula 2.
>   Variation 2.1
>   Variation 2.2, *ad infinitum.*

Unfortunately, in the aforementioned quest for the "look of science," a steadily increasing number of research reports have had tables and figures numbered in the above fashion—inappropriately!

Rule. Tables, figures, *i.e.*, graphs, charts, pictures, illustrations of any sort — should be used *only* when: 1) they are a natural product of the data; 2) they clarify the data; and 3) their production was the stated, primary purpose of the research.

Rule. To the extent possible, all forms of illustrative material should be placed in context with the narrative and should precede, if feasible, any explanatory discussion.

Comment. Because of the inflexibility of the typewritten manuscript, some leeway is permitted in the placement of illustrative material; leeway, not license! In printed matter, the tendency has grown to present pictures in what is termed "a gallery," *i.e.*, a sheaf of pictures interspersed at various places in the book, or appended at the back of the book. That procedure is counter-indicated in scholarly work. *Put the illustration as close to the apposite text as possible.*

Rule. No matter what form of illustrative material is being used, *specified margins must be maintained!*

Tables

Rule. Numbers of and headings for tables appear *above* them. Explanations of internal notation, symbols, or legends appear immediately *below* a table. The source of the table, if it was taken from another work or based on data from another work, is documented in a footnote. Copyright laws must be observed for illustrations as well as for text.

Rule. If your paper is to have a considerable number of tables, it would be well to use Arabic numbers. If you plan to use only a few tables, Roman numbers should be used.

Examples

Table I
Analysis of Variance Source Table for Sociability[1]

Variations	degrees of freedom	sum of squares	mean square	F
Subject Groups	1	3354	3354	101.02*
Schools	4	198	49.5	1.53
Interaction	4	50	12.5	0.388
Errors	70	2256	32.2	
Totals	79	5858		

* Significant $p < .05$.

[1] Francine Silverblank, "Sense of Responsibility, Level of Anxiety, and Sociability in Suburban Male High School Seniors Who Are Talented in Mathematics and Those Talented in English," unpublished dissertation for the Ed.D., New York University, 1970, 63.

Table II
Data for the Analysis of Variance of the Variance in Anxiety for Students Talented in English[1]

f	x	fx	$(x-\bar{x})$	$(x-\bar{x})^2$	$f(x-\bar{x})^2$
1	19	19	12.6	158.76	158.76
3	20	60	11.6	134.56	403.68
1	23	23	8.6	73.96	73.96
4	24	96	7.6	57.76	231.04
4	25	100	6.6	43.56	174.24
2	27	54	4.6	21.16	42.32
1	28	28	3.6	12.96	12.96
3	30	90	1.6	2.56	7.68
1	31	31	.6	.36	.36
2	32	64	.4	.16	.32
1	33	33	1.4	1.96	1.96

(continued on page 51)

[1] Francine Silverblank, "Sense of Responsibility, Level of Anxiety, and Sociability in Suburban Male High School Seniors Who Are Talented in Mathematics and Those Talented in English," unpublished dissertation for the Ed.D., New York University, 1970, 115.

Table II (continued)

Data for the Analysis of Variance of the
Variance in Anxiety for Students
Talented in English[1]

f	x	fx	$(x-\bar{x})$	$(x-\bar{x})^2$	$f(x-\bar{x})^2$
3	34	102	2.4	5.76	17.28
3	35	105	3.4	11.56	34.68
3	36	108	4.4	19.36	58.08
1	40	40	8.4	70.56	70.56
2	41	82	9.4	88.36	176.72
1	42	42	10.4	108.16	108.16
1	44	44	12.4	153.16	153.76
2	48	98	16.4	268.96	537.92
1	47	47	15.4	237.16	237.16
40		1264			2501.60

$$\bar{x} = \frac{\Sigma fx}{\Sigma f} = \frac{1264}{40} = 31.6 \qquad \sigma^2 = \frac{\Sigma f(x-\bar{x})^2}{f-1} = \frac{2501.60}{39} = 64.14$$

[1] *Ibid.*

Comment. If you had actually used several tables from the same source sequentially, you would have used *Ibid.* to identify the source and the appropriate pages.

Rule. When a table has to be divided, no narrative should intervene between the successive sections of the table.

Reduction of Tables, Charts, Graphs

If any table, chart, or graph is exceedingly large and detailed, but it seems imperative that it be on one page, it is possible to have it typed in extra large (billboard) type. It may, then, through photocopy process, be reduced to fit within prescribed margins on an 8½" x 11" page. However, if the reduction process would make the data difficult to read, it should *not* be used. Divide the table; clarity of communication is preeminent.

Table III

Gordon Personal Profile Scores for Responsibility and Their Corresponding Percentile Ranks by Schools and Subject Area[1]

Subject Groups		A		B		SCHOOLS C		D		E	
		Score	0/0	Score	0/0	Score	0/0	Score	0/0	Score	0/0
ENGLISH		25	74	19	31	21	45	23	60	18	24
		25	74	23	60	24	67	26	80	25	74
		26	80	26	80	25	74	26	80	26	80
		28	89	28	89	25	74	26	80	27	85
		29	93	30	95	26	80	28	89	28	89
		29	93	31	97	27	85	30	95	29	93
		32	98	32	98	28	89	31	97	30	95
		34	100	36	100	29	93	36	100	31	97
MATHEMATICS		26	80	21	45	23	60	23	60	20	38
		26	80	24	67	23	60	26	80	26	80
		27	85	25	74	24	67	27	85	26	80
		29	93	27	85	26	80	28	89	27	85
		30	95	27	85	26	80	29	93	28	89
		31	97	33	99	30	95	31	97	28	89
		33	99	34	100	30	95	33	99	29	93
		33	99	42	100	32	98	35	100	32	98

[1] Francine Silverblank, "Sense of Responsibility, Level of Anxiety, and Sociability in Suburban Male High School Seniors Who Are Talented in Mathematics and Those Talented in English," unpublished dissertation for the Ed.D, New York University, 1970, 65.

Note that Table III could not be displayed horizontally and was thus inserted lengthwise.

Rule. Illustrations may be inserted lengthwise, but the top of each illustration *must* be at the binding side. Illustrations may *not* be spread across left and right pages; fold-outs may *not* be used in Masters' theses or doctoral dissertations.

Figures and Illustrations

All of the strictures described for tables apply to the use of charts, graphs, figures of any kind, with the exception of the placement of number and caption.

Rule. Numbers (Arabic, in this instance) and captions for charts, graphs, and figures of any kind, appear *below* them. Explanations of internal notation, symbols, or legends may appear in the body of the illustration or immediately below it. If the source of the illustration is another work, it must be documented in a footnote. Copyright laws must be observed.

Examples

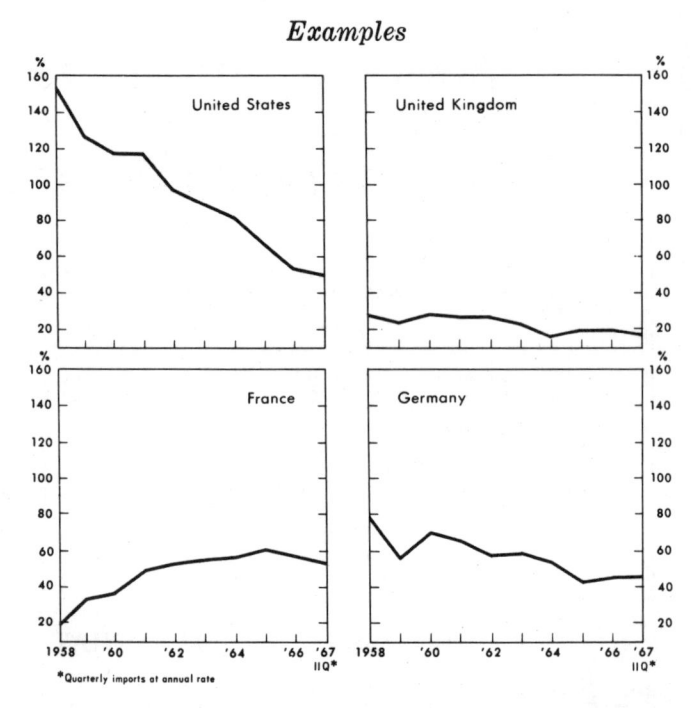

Fig. 1. Reserves As Per Cent of Annual Imports for Selected Countries

---

[1] Source: International Monetary Fund, in *Road Maps of Industry*, No. 1583, New York: National Industrial Conference Board, December 1, 1967.

Comment. In an actual manuscript, the footnote would be at the foot of the page. Discussion or another figure might intervene.

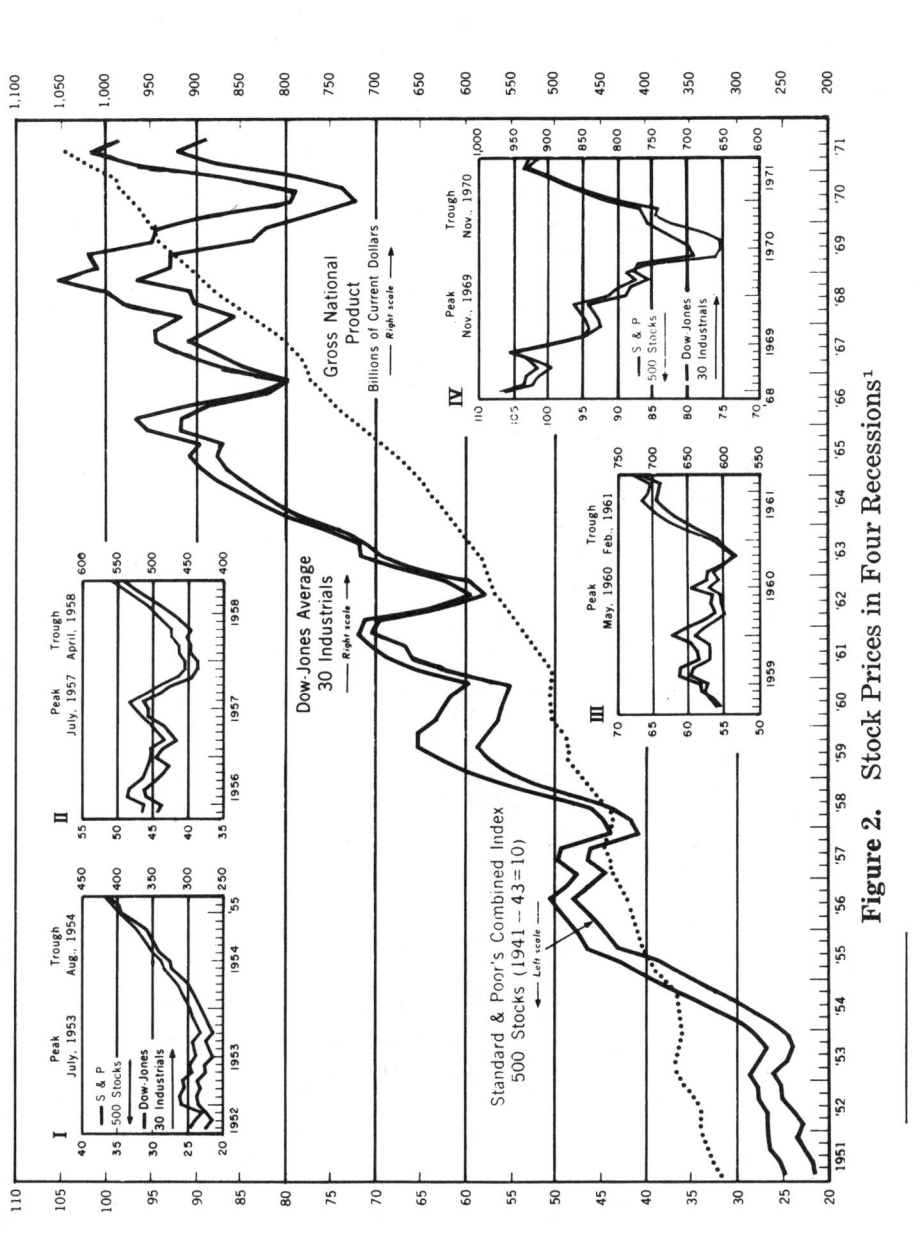

Figure 2. Stock Prices in Four Recessions[1]

[1] "The Stock Market and the Economy," *Road Maps of Industry*, No. 1677, New York: The National Industrial Conference Board, November 1, 1971.

60 / *The Writer's Handbook*

There are many forms of illustrations. Your work might require several bars of music, a cartoon, caricature, a photograph, a print of a slide, or a print of a painting.

Rule. Whenever reproductions of paintings, etchings, sculptures, etc. are used, the actual size of the original should be specified. This may be done directly beneath the caption, or it may be included in the list of illustrations in the bibliography.

Rule. Illustrations should be assigned Arabic numerals for ease of reference. Number and caption for illustrations appear *below*. When a reproduction is used, supply the date.

Comment. Any information which will help the reader to perceive the original should be provided.

1. Tibetan Figure[1]
8" x 10" — black and white.

---

[1] Tibetan figure representing Ts'on-K'a-pa. Cloisonne enamel on copper, various colors, yellow predominating. K'ang Hsi period (1662-1722). The Metropolitan Museum of Art, New York.

2. *The Mini-and-Maxi Era* by Herblock, 1969[1]

---

[1] Herblock, "The Mini-and-Maxi Era," cartoon in Herblock's *State of the Union,* New York: Simon and Schuster, 1973, 43.

Reduction of Illustrations

It is frequently necessary to use reductions of photographs, paintings, 35mm prints and slides. In the case of the last two, it is possible to have them reproduced on an 8½" x 11" sheet of photographic paper called a "contact sheet." They are produced in strips, 15 or 20 to a sheet. Remember: Specified margins must be maintained.

CHAPTER VII
The Term Paper

There are two prime considerations in writing a term paper — the teacher[i] and you. It is impossible to anticipate the eccentricities of every teacher. Some require you to use a particular kind of paper and to place your name in a special place on each page; some will accept only a typed manuscript; some want the paper encased in a particular binder. Discretion dictates that you bow to these little oddities.

More difficult is the great disparity among teachers in decreeing the length of papers. Some, regardless of the profundity of the topic, limit the length to ten pages. Don't write eleven! But don't choose a topic worthy of a 1,000-page volume. Some require tomes, regardless of the triviality of the topic. You have a choice: 1) Be a hypocrite and pad the data with excessive verbiage; or 2) Be a rebel and try to argue the teacher into some respectable composition of your divergent views of the importance of the subject.

It is hoped that the advice which follows is based on a rational approach to writing about subjects of genuine worth. Some exceptions to that happy end are discussed here — not all.

The Teacher, The Topic and You

Unfortunately, teachers do frequently assign what you consider banal, inane topics. Some teachers are open to suggestion, and you may be able to request permission to write on a topic more compatible with your interests. A few judicious cautions follow.

Caution 1. Try to find out through the student grapevine if the particular teacher: 1) says "yes" to a suggestion, but judges such work more harshly;

---

[i] The word "teacher" may be read "professor" throughout this chapter, if it makes you feel better.

2) says "no" and remembers that you "questioned his authority," and is punitive in the reading of such papers; and 3) really accepts such suggestions honestly and judges the work on the basis of reasonable criteria. If the teacher seems to fit "1" or "2" and you persist, don't complain if you have a difficult time.

Caution 2. If the teacher fits "3," it does not necessarily follow that you can choose some insipid topic about which you *think* you know something. When you propose an alternative topic, be able to provide the teacher with sufficient evidence that you have done some careful preliminary research and that you *know* there are sufficient data to warrant a paper. You might cite several sources you have already explored and know to be available in an accessible library. If you succeed in getting permission to deviate from the regular assignment and do a shoddy job, you're a fool! In addition, his experience with you might cause the teacher to refuse such leeway to any other student.

Caution 3. When the topic is one of your own choosing, whether by special dispensation or because that is routine procedure, do not take off into outer space, either figuratively or literally. Choose a topic with which you have at least a glancing acquaintance and, preferably, a little knowledge. Obviously, if you are to learn something — and it is rumored that that is one of the purposes for which you are in school — you should select a topic about which there are things you do not know. *Do not* — especially if you are a slow reader and a tortured writer— engage yourself with a topic that is completely virgin territory to you.

Caution 4. If you *are* a slow reader or a tortured writer, or both: 1) if the teacher does not assign the term paper topic within the first two weeks, try to see him, explain your difficulty and ask for some advance knowledge of the assignment so that you may get an early start; and 2) if necessary, *trap yourself* into getting that early start. Use any device you can think of and enlist the aid of your friends and relatives into pushing you to start the research *and* the writing as early as possible.

Caution 5. No matter how "exciting" or "challenging" a topic may seem to you, take a *very* careful survey of: 1) how much actual time you have before the due date for the paper; 2) how much research will be required to do a creditable paper; and 3) how many other term papers will be due at about the same time. A good subject deserves better than superficial treatment. You may be able to slice off one portion of the topic you initially selected and produce a thoroughly researched paper on that segment. If the topic is not divisible, you might better set it aside for a course or a semester when you have more time, more skill, and fewer demands upon your resources. It is wiser to do less and do it in superior fashion than to commit yourself to a goal you cannot possibly achieve. On the other hand, it is worth stretching occasionally and reaching for a star.

Caution 6. Having heeded all of the above advice (especially Caution 4), if you find you are having serious difficulty in securing sufficient data or in writing about the topic because it has proved antipathetic to your thinking or not within your critical competence, don't just sit there. No one is going to wave a magic wand and make your troubles evaporate. Nor after two or three earnest attempts to cope with it, should you just plod on, particularly if you know whatever you have produced is puerile and poor. Go back to the teacher and ask permission to select another topic, bearing with you the evidence of your genuine efforts. If you have made an early start, there should be time to do all that is needed for a different topic more in keeping with your knowledge and skill.

Oddly enough, teachers are people and just as subject to quixotic shifts as anyone else. You may only conjecture about the personality, idiosyncrasies, and behavior patterns of your teachers. You should be able to get to *know* your own abilities, bounds, flexibility, and potential for growth, if you address yourself seriously to such personal measurement. Self-knowledge and self-evaluation will be useful, not only during your school years, but also throughout your life. Regular review, reevaluation, and reconstruction of your own competence is an intrinsic aid[i] both for your professional and private life — as long as you do not carry introspection to the point where it immobilizes you.

If you are a ring-tailed wonder, a veritable genius, so adjudicated by a Board of Geniuses, ignore all of the above.

Procedures

Having gone through all of the prescribed diplomacy and soul-searching recommended, you now have accepted or selected a topic.

The Title

Do not linger over the title. Dash it off! Students have been known to spend weeks "composing" a "clever" title, to the detriment of their research and writing. It is a ploy similar to the too frequent trips to the refrigerator while you "think." You will have opportunity to revise the title or scrap it for another. The best time to produce the title is after the paper is completed and you really know what it is about.

---

[i] If it was good enough for Plato and John Dewey, it might be good enough for you.

The Descriptive Sentence or Paragraph

Construct a sentence or, if necessary, a paragraph which describes your intention and incorporates the full meaning of your tentative title. Take a look at the prefaces of two or three good books. Many authors provide a paragraph or two of "fair warning," in which they tell the reader precisely what their purposes were. Some even define what they did *not* intend to do. Your descriptive paragraph is largely for your edification. It is the initial step in mapping the course of your journey through this particular paper.

Even if the assignment is one of those deadly ones like "Do a précis of one book selected from the first ten titles of the bibliography," the descriptive paragraph is a good device. Occasionally you are required to do a whole series of "busywork" book reports of that boring nature. If your academic aspirations are genuine, *i.e.*, you mean to learn something, the descriptive paragraph for each brief paper should help you drain more substance from the books than a cursory recapitulation of their contents.

Examples

1. Title: Existentialism: Camus *vs.* Sartre

Descriptive Paragraph: The similarities and differences between the concepts of existentialism of Camus and Sartre will be explored, described, and evaluated. Reference will also be made to the possibility of indebtedness of either or both to Kierkegaard.

Comment. You have committed yourself to an extremely interesting but difficult and demanding endeavor. You may find that you have neither the time nor the competence to deal with Kierkegaard. You may also find that an exploration of the existential theory of either Camus or Sartre is a big enough chore for you to handle. At this stage, you know what your objectives are. You may be forced to pull in your lines later.

2. Title: Napier and the Development of Logarithms

Descriptive Paragraph: A brief biography of Napier will be provided as well as a history of the development of logarithms and the logarithmic tables. The practical application of logs to bookkeeping problems will be exemplified.

Comment. You know what your immediate goals are. If you are planning a career as a teacher of mathematics, this paper might later prove useful in teaching the less gifted, non-math major.

The Work Plan

With your title and descriptive paragraph clutched in your hot little hand, get yourself to the library and head for the card files. You are supposed to have learned how to use a library in elementary school. You may have been absent, it may never have been taught or you may have forgotten.

Do not hesitate to ask the librarian to instruct you. If you approach one with dyspepsia, find another one. Librarians are usually delighted to give you the best possible information on the use of the library, since it relieves them of having to fetch for you over and over again.

It is not possible to deal with every potential topic, discipline, or personal writing style. The technique shown above for dealing with a topic may be generalized from to apply to an infinite variety of topics, an infinite variety of courses, and an infinite variety of personal writing styles. The descriptive, instructive material which follows will deal with two quite different topics for illustrative purposes. Though the topics are literary and theological, the "advice" is sound for the construction of a paper on anything which is subject to investigation.

First Term Paper Topic

1. Title: Shakespeare's Characterization of the Mature Woman in *A Midsummer Night's Dream* and *Hamlet*

Descriptive Paragraph: Hippolyta in *A Midsummer Night's Dream* and Gertrude in *Hamlet* will be analyzed on the basis of what they say, what is said to them and, if possible, what is said about them within the plays. Critical literature on Shakespeare's building of character, in both comedy and tragedy, and on his treatment of women will be studied. Recent literature on Shakespeare's portrayal of women, as well as the classical Shakespearean critical material, will be explored.

Search of the Card Files

You should read at least two editions of each play, *e.g.*, The Tudor and The Temple, with their critical notes, especially anything pertaining to Hippolyta and Gertrude. If your library has a facsimile of the Folio edition of each play, read it. The Variorum edition would be helpful, too. Since there are an infinite number of editions of Shakespeare's works, unless you have access to other libraries, you will have to depend on what your own library has. Beware of abridged editions! Bear in mind that you must not assume that a word with which you think you are familiar had precisely the same meaning in Shakespeare's day. If you make judgments on the basis of your definition, rather than on that of Elizabethan England, your judgments may be erroneous.

You will want to do some reading of a climate-setting nature. Marchette Chute's *Shakespeare of London*,[i] Anthony Burgess's novel *Nothing Like*

---

[i] Marchette Chute, *Shakespeare of London*, New York: E. P. Dutton and Co., Inc., 1949.

the Sun,[i] the novel by Colin MacInnes, *Three Years to Play*,[ii] and Burgess's handsomely illustrated *Shakespeare*,[iii] coupled with Algernon Charles Swinburne's eloquent introductory essay to the Oxford edition,[iv] all should put you in tune.

The critical literature on Shakespeare is abundant. You and only you will know how much you are capable of reading, absorbing, and writing in the time between the beginning of your research and the date the paper is due. You might adopt one of several means to circumscribe the extent of your research: 1) read criticism written over the years from the 17th century to the present, selecting one notable critical work from each century; 2) select five British and five American critics of eminence; or 3) concentrate on critics of the 20th century only. These are only examples of possible ways to establish limits for your research.

Critiques of Shakespeare's attitude toward women may be found in the literature discussed above and in more recent "women's liberation" publications. You will want to consult journals, magazines and monographs of the movement as well as the various publications by such notables as Germaine Greer,[v] Kate Millett,[vi] Betty Friedan,[vii] *et al.*

Second Term Paper Topic

2. Title: A Comparison of the Theologies of Martin Luther and John Calvin

Descriptive Paragraph: A survey will be made of the theologies of Luther and Calvin. Their theories will be set in biographical context. Special emphasis will be placed on the distinction between their views on predestination.

Once again you are confronted with an almost overwhelming quantity

---

[i] Anthony Burgess, *Nothing Like the Sun,* New York: W. W. Norton and Co., 1964.

[ii] Colin MacInnes, *Three Years to Play,* New York: Farrar, Straus and Giroux, Inc., 1970.

[iii] Anthony Burgess, *Shakespeare,* New York: Alfred A. Knopf, 1970.

[iv] Algernon Charles Swinburne, "General Introduction," to *The Comedies of Shakespeare, The Histories and Poems of Shakespeare, The Tragedies of Shakespeare,* the text of the Oxford edition prepared by W. J. Craig, 3 vols., London: Oxford University Press, 1952, in *The Comedies of Shakespeare,* I, v-xxxvi.

[v] Germaine Greer, *The Female Eunuch,* New York: McGraw-Hill Book Company, Inc., 1971.

[vi] Kate Millett, *Sexual Politics,* New York: Doubleday & Company, Inc., 1971.

[vii] Betty Friedan, *The Feminine Mystique,* New York: W. W. Norton and Co., 1963.

of literature. You will, of course, want to read as much as possible of the original material by both men, *e.g.*, Luther's "Table Talk," replies by him to questions posed at his table and noted by his disciples; Calvin's *Institutes of the Christian Religion*, etc.

With this topic, you have the added problem of being watchful for bias, *e.g.*, if you read books about Luther by Lutheran theologians only, they will provide insufficient data for a sound piece of research. The books of Roland Bainton, *e.g.*, *Here I Stand*,[i] are well researched, but they are the product of a Lutheran, and some of them are published by Lutheran presses, *e.g.*, *Women of the Reformation*,[ii] Erik Erikson's *Young Man Luther*[iii] is a psychological biography, but you might want to know what Erikson's theological training was. Stefan Zweig's *Castellio gegen Calvin* is available in English under the title *Right to Heresy; Castellio against Calvin*,[iv] and Erich Fromm's *Psychoanalysis and Religion*[v] does some of the things for Calvin that Erikson did for Luther. The way in which both men are treated in the *Catholic Encyclopedia* might provide a partial antidote to bias in authors who are communicants of either denomination.

In dealing with the literature mentioned for either topic, one or two, or any other topic, it is imperative that you acknowledge the fact that you are using some resources which are fiction or semifiction. This would apply to plays, novels, and short stories. This should not prevent you from using such material, especially if written by authors known to be careful researchers. To aid you in establishing the reliability of authors of historical novels, plays *et al.*, read the reviews in responsible literary journals or book review sections of newspapers. The play about Luther[vi] — which drew heavily on Erikson's book — Zweig's work and the novels by Burgess and MacInnes fall into this category.

Taking Notes [vii]

Bear in mind two dicta: 1) Try to limit the amount of direct quotation you copy to those phrases or sentences or paragraphs which have most bear-

---

[i] Roland H. Bainton, *Here I Stand: A Life of Martin Luther*, New York: Abingdon-Cokesbury Press, 1951.

[ii] Roland H. Bainton, *Women of the Reformation*, Minneapolis, Minnesota: Augsburg Publishing House, 1971.

[iii] Erik Erickson, *Young Man Luther*, New York: W. W. Norton and Co., 1958.

[iv] Stefan Zweig, *Right to Heresy; Castellio against Calvin*, trans. by Eden and Cedar Paul, Boston: Beacon Press, 1951.

[v] Erich Fromm, *Psychoanalysis and Religion*, New Haven: Yale University Press, 1951.

[vi] John Osborne, *Luther, A Play*, New York: Criterion Books, 1961.

[vii] Read Chapter I very carefully.

ing on your topic and which are so eloquently written as to prohibit your attempting to paraphrase them. The other cause for using direct quotation is brash generalization or statements by the author which differ radically from the usual point of view. You will want to be especially careful to quote such statements with accuracy. And 2) If you own the book, do *not* delude yourself by underscoring seemingly significant passages. (This applies, too, when you are studying an assignment or for an examination.) You *think* you will remember what you have underscored, or you *think* you will have time to go back and reread all of those passages before writing the paper (or taking the examination). You won't! It is important to ask yourself, as you read, what is truly significant, salient, or apposite about the passage. If you have an apt answer, either copy or paraphrase the nugget of thought most pertinent to your purpose, not the entire lode.

Whether you quote directly or paraphrase, you *must* acknowledge the source in a footnote.[i]

In working with the actual speeches of Hippolyta and Gertrude, or with other dialogue in the two plays, and in working with the original materials of Luther and Calvin, explore every nuance and meaning. If, as suggested, you read several editions, you may want to include commentary on certain specific passages from all of your sources. However, if practicable, you might establish at the very outset that you will use one edition as your standard source for quotation throughout the paper. In that case, you may so state in a footnote on the first page of the paper.

Example

---

[1] Unless otherwise stipulated, all quotations from both *A Midsummer Night's Dream* and *Hamlet* are from the New Variorum edition, edited by Horace Howard Furness, 27 vols., Philadelphia: J. B. Lippincott Company, 1871-1940, *A Midsummer Night's Dreame*, 1923, X, *Hamlet*, 1918, III-IV.

You would do well to choose an edition which makes it possible for you to obtain each play in a separate, portable volume; in some of the editions you may find the tragedies in one volume, the comedies in another, and the poems in a third.

The Outline

When you have done an exhaustive search of material in the card files and have completed a "first round" of reading, you should have the elements for a rough outline of the paper.

---

[i] Read Chapters III and IV very carefully.

I. A Survey of the Critical Literature of Shakespeare's Technique of Character Development and Delineation
II. Examination of the Character of Hippolyta
III. Examination of the Character of Gertrude
IV. Comparison of Hippolyta and Gertrude
V. Survey of the Critical Literature of the Past on Shakespeare's Portrayal of Women
VI. Survey of Modern Critical Literature on Shakespeare's Portrayal of Women
VII. Examination of Hippolyta and Gertrude in the Light of V and VI.

There is an important VIII, too, but for the time being the above is a guide for sorting your notes. Separate your note cards in accordance with the topics above. When notes seem applicable to more than one topic, insert a cross-reference card,[i] *e.g.*, you have a card headed "Swinburne" filed under topic II, but it applies also to topic III; insert a card under III marked, "See II, Swinburne, card 4."

Writing the Paper

Opening Paragraph

You may or may not be able to use your original descriptive paragraph as an opener. Even if it does not seem completely appropriate, don't sit there brooding over it. You can always go back and insert a different statement. Copy the one you have! You need something to get you started and that paragraph is available. At a later time, you may use part of it, rewrite it, or scrap it entirely and start fresh. The important thing is to get moving. Just be sure to reread that first paragraph when the paper is completed. You'll want to have complied with the "contract" you made with your reader.

First Draft

Using your outline as your guide, write a first draft of the paper. Triple space, whether typing or handwriting. Do *not* write your conclusion and do *not* linger over phrases or sentences! Referring constantly to your assembled research data, and *supplying all footnotes in accurate detail*,[ii] WRITE!

---

[i] See Chapter I, 3.

[ii] See Chapter IV.

If you are typing and find it difficult to figure footnote space, write footnotes on a lined pad and tape them onto the page. Bear in mind that there are 65 spaces on each 8½" x 11" page, which is standard-size typing paper. You must maintain margins.[i] Six spaces must be kept free for the required margin at the bottom of the page.

Number each page in the upper right corner so that you may refer to the proper page when you start to edit the first draft. Pagination of a term paper may be in the upper right corner. (This does not apply to a Master's thesis or a doctoral dissertation.)

Each paragraph should be built in a logical, sequential fashion and each section should have its own logical sequence. Sometimes, if you have assembled your note cards with care, even a first draft will have this ordered structure. If it does not, you may alter, delete, amend, or rewrite paragraphs and sections.

Second Draft

Careful planning of your time should make it possible to put the entire draft aside for at least one day. When you return to it, try to read it as though someone else had written it, and begin your editorial work. Occasionally you will find that some material from each section should be culled and used as part of your heretofore not considered section VIII. It will be an analytical, critical, evaluative conclusion. Sometimes a paragraph at the beginning, middle, or end of your first draft appears to fit better someplace else. You may find that you have written almost precisely the same thing in two places, either within a section or in different sections. Select the better written one and place it where it does the most good. Delete the other.

You may find that you want to combine two sections, *e.g.*, V and VI in the sample outline. You *cannot* just delete the heading or headings. It will be necessary to do some rewriting to blend the material and to produce a new ordered, logical internal sequence under a newly devised heading.

To facilitate your editing, do not rewrite or retype unless absolutely necessary. Cut and paste. Having triple spaced, you have room to add connective phrases or sentences. If more extensive writing seems indicated, allow space when you paste. *Move footnotes when you move sentences or paragraphs.* This edited version of your draft may be moderately messy with pages that are uneven in length, but the actual cutting and pasting should be done with care so that text and footnotes travel together.

When the surgery has been completed, read straight through the paper again, adding, deleting, polishing, and striving for clear, well-developed and interestingly expressed ideas. Check to be sure that you have paid proper obeisance to sources of ideas other than your own and have backed up your own ideas with responsible evidence. It is not enough to say, "I feel . . ."

---

[i] See Chapter III, 21.

or, if you are required to use the third person, "The writer feels . . ." Your feelings are not a matter of concern. What you *think* and *why* you think it are going to be evaluated. Take notes as you read for use in section VIII.

Concluding Section

Ideally, having done this post-operative cautery, you should be able to do another complete reading and polishing. In reality, it is unlikely that you will have time, especially if you have several term papers to do. Whether you have time to reread or not, now is the time to do your concluding section: analytical, critical, evaluative. It is at this stage that what you have learned from your research will be revealed. Try to take time to reflect upon all of the material, the ideas expressed by "experts," the reasoning and data they supplied to support their points of view. If you agree, you will want to provide the reader with information about how your thinking developed and your rationale for agreement. Be equally, if not more, lucid about your disagreements. Exert care to supply the bases in *knowledge* (not emotion) and reflection for the disparity in your view from that of "authority."

The conclusion of your paper should deal with all of the highlights of the particular sections and should then present a synthesis of the various parts, emphasizing truly significant ideas and concepts. There should be a final evaluative sentence or paragraph to pull the strings and close the curtain.

Reread your entire concluding section and subject it to the same incisive editorial work. Remember that, although the reading and research are important, the most revelatory part of the paper is the way in which you have digested the data and turned it into an integrated part of your knowledge.

Final Copy

When you are satisfied with the last section, take a look at that opening paragraph or two and, if necessary, rewrite. This is also the time to make up your mind about the title. If the original title is no longer descriptive of the paper, write a new one.

If you have inserted accurate footnotes as you composed the paper, putting together your bibliography should be a simple task.[i] Any appendixes necessary to the completion of the paper should be carefully assembled now so that you have a complete manuscript from which to type.[ii]

Now — write or type the entire paper. Proofread it as carefully as possible for errors in spelling, grammar or diction (choice of appropriate

---

[i] See Chapter V.

[ii] See Chapter III, "Pagination," 21–22.

word or words). If you are lucky, you will have a relative or friend who is willing to proofread it for you after you have done a fastidious job. Few people are completely successful proofreaders of their own material.

No one can guarantee you an "A," but the procedure described, if conscientiously adhered to — even in part — should assure that writing a term paper will have fulfilled its purpose, *i.e.*, it will have been "a learning experience."

CHAPTER VIII

The Doctoral Dissertation and the Master's Thesis

Many of the precepts inherent in writing a term paper obtain in the planning and execution of a Master's thesis or a doctoral dissertation of any type, *e.g.*, Ph.D., Ed.D., D.S.W. With each step up the strata of degrees, the demand for quality and profundity grows and so does the number and variety of persons to whom you must answer.

Initially, you have three important concerns: 1) yourself; 2) your subject; and 3) someone with insight and experience in your discipline with whom to discuss you and your subject. A lover or a friend may be supportive, but what they offer will be useful later. Right now you need someone with knowledge about and interest in you and the subject; someone to ask you penetrating, nagging questions. Whether you have only the glimmer of an idea or a full-blown topic, every positive and negative aspect should be explored, dissected.

When you are ready to approach this informed person, write a statement, no matter how rough, of what you wish to do. It will provide him with a springboard for discourse and will force you to try to express your notion well.

No one, neither you nor your sounding board, will be able to anticipate all of the pitfalls, strange encounters, frustrations, detours, and delights which lurk in the future. Intelligent anticipation, however, may obviate much grief and many obstructions.

The Subject and You

You may spend a year or more "going steady" with your dissertation (sometimes, unfortunately, even longer). The most dearly beloved of human beings occasionally evokes anger, disgust, boredom. A dissertation subject does not have nearly as many compensatory attributes. You had better have a genuine passion for it and the mode of research it requires in order to discipline yourself through the tedious hours, the seemingly persnickety demands of your sponsor(s), the moments of despair, and the petty requirements of your department and university.[i] Keep reminding yourself that many other abused, even less talented candidates not only survived, but also triumphed.

Choosing a Topic

In some institutions and especially in some departments, you have little choice in the selection of a topic. Overtly or covertly, you are steered by the chairman of the department, your academic advisor or the professor in whose special subject you have majored toward a topic dear to his heart and near to his own current research. If the topic pleases, you are to be congratulated. If the topic is antipathetic to your nature: 1) you should have discovered it long before you reached the subject selection stage and, unless you are willing to go elsewhere and start all over again, you had best make peace with reality; 2) you may wish to make a major issue of it and, if you are lucky, your argument may prevail; but you may be asked to leave and, thereby, be forced to abandon your doctorate, or start all over again elsewhere; 3) you might try a few political ploys for wooing the person who holds the reins of power to let you add a dash of your own seasoning or even to expand the topic decreed by at least one section more challenging or interesting or compatible with your academic and professional goals; and 4) you may just have to put your desires in escrow for the duration and swat away at completing your research as quickly as possible, so that you may get on with your life's work.

Regardless of the circumstances that have led to the topic which has been approved, there are certain important cautions to bear in mind.

Caution 1. *It is imperative* that the subject be one for which you have not only an affinity, but also the appropriate academic equipment. Disaster awaits the candidate who essays research for which he lacks some essential knowledge or skill. The disaster may be academic, *e.g.*, after weeks or months of work, he finds that he lacks competence and has to abandon the subject; or it may be economic, *e.g.*, because of lack of knowledge and/or skill, he must hire a consultant for a considerable fee to extricate him from his predicament. Do not delude yourself! If statistical manipulation is a part of your planned research, you are not going to waken some morning

---

[i] "My grandfather was watching a man watering the street. It was raining. He said to the man: *'Mon ami, pourquoi arrosez-vous la rue qu'il pleut?'* ['My friend, why do you wash the street when it is raining?'] To which the man in charge of the watering cart replied with a withering look. *'Sachez, monsieur, que la pluie est un phénomène naturel et que l'arrosage est un phenomene administratif.'* ['Don't you know that the rain is a natural phenomenon and washing the streets is an administrative one.']" Sir John Pollock, cited in Jeremy Fisher, *Lambe's Tale*, London: Chatto & Windus, 1969, "Spring," 7.

76 / The Writer's Handbook

and find yourself transformed into a wizard in statistics. Learn the techniques *and* the underlying principles. The consultant will not be on hand to rescue you when you are defending your dissertation. The alternative is to scrap the topic for which you are not equipped and find one for which you are.

Caution 2. *It is imperative* that you determine whether the topic has already been researched. The professors in your department or another one who specialize in the subject should be familiar with current research. Ask them, but do not rely on their knowledge alone. Scour the indexes of research in the field; read the lists, if available in the subject, of dissertations in process; plow through the learned jonrnals, monographs, and texts; examine the pertinent years in *Dissertation Abstracts*[i] and, with the advice and assistance of a librarian familiar with the process, apply to University Microfilms for a Datrix search for completed dissertations which appear to be similar or related to your topic.[ii] Don't panic if you find a title or an abstract that appears to have dealt with your proposed research. Neither the topic nor the abstract tells the whole story. Get the dissertation itself, either through interlibrary loan or in microfilm. Even if it is very much like what you had in mind, there may be a different approach or an extension of what has been done which you may investigate.

Caution 3. *It is imperative* that, before you become irrevocably addicted to the one topic, you obtain the approval of a member of your department capable of assuming that responsibility, or willing to help you get approval from a committee which is vested with power of approval in your institution. This may or may not be the person you first pestered and may or may not be the person who will be your dissertation sponsor. (More about sponsors later.) For this step it is even more important that you have a written statement of what you hope to do — that is, to what question you are seeking an answer. You cannot expect anyone to spend time and energy to assist you if you arrive with some diffuse maunderings. Get the topic in writing with as much clarity as possible.

---

[i] Published by Xerox Education Group, University Microfilms, Ann Arbor, Michigan. Originally issued as *Microfilm Abstracts*, vols. 1-11, 1938-1951; then as *Dissertation Abstracts*, vols. 12-29, 1952-1969; and now, *Dissertation Abstracts International*, published monthly in two parts: A. The Humanities and Social Sciences; and B. Science and Engineering, *e.g.*, *Dissertation Abstracts International, November*, 1972, 33:5A.

[ii] The librarians may prove to be your most valuable friends. Treat them with courtesy and respect and you will have reason to be grateful to them for the rest of your life. Sometimes one librarian is assigned the task of assisting doctoral candidates. Whether he is so assigned or whether he is a regular librarian, he will be able to direct you to the appropriate resources for such a hunt and should have the forms for applying for the *DATRIX* search. *DATRIX*, University Microfilms, P.O. Box 1764, Ann Arbor, Michigan, 48106.

If you have any qualms about all the work for Caution 2, remember that every bit of reading you do on or related to your topic may be and frequently is useful to you in doing the actual dissertation research and writing.

Scope of the Research

There are two more items related to you and the subject which must be considered. One, the need for or the significance of the study (to be discussed later). The other, the size or scope of the research (to be dealt with now).

It would be both salutary and miraculous if every doctoral dissertation made a genuine contribution to knowledge. Most of them, sadly, are exercises in one or another discipline and form of research. Some of them rearrange previously known data in new, imaginative patterns. A few of them add information (facts) to an already considerable body of knowledge. Too many of them are repetitions, perhaps with minor differences, of other research;[i] slight changes in locale, age, sex, economic status, ethnic origin, or number of subjects may be all that differentiates one piece of research from another. The ability to replicate research in the pure sciences is laudable. Replication of research in the social sciences, when carefully designed to guard against repetition for repetition's sake, may make a worthy contribution. However, the interminable trial of a particular instrument, because it was created and tested by "reputable researchers," may be a prime example of academic doodling and futility.

On the other hand, do not make the mistake of believing that your dissertation must be unique and must make an earthshaking contribution to knowledge. Try to preserve some semblance of initiative and imagination, but do not count on writing something that the whole scholarly world is panting for and do not expect publishers to hound you with promises of best-seller listing and tons of money. If your sponsors, the examiners at your defense of your dissertation, and your mother actually read it, rest content.

Some universities limit the length of the proposal for the dissertation and the dissertation itself; others have no such restrictions.[ii] You *must* limit the size and scope of the research yourself. If you do not, you may be researching and writing forever. In the interim, your sponsors may have retired or died and the academic life of your credits may have expired.

---

[i] *E.g.*, "One cannot help wondering whether everything important to discover in the field of lasers might not have been discovered just as fast with only 40 projects, with the other 360 groups doing something less repetitious." John R. Platt, *Perception and Change, Projections for Survival*, Ann Arbor: The University of Michigan Press, 1970, 4.

[ii] Hereinafter all references will be to departmental requirements. It is assumed that you will know whether the rules by which you must abide are, in fact, departmental, divisional, school-wide, or imposed by the university as a whole.

You should not consider your dissertation your *magnum opus*. It is the means whereby you will achieve academic respectability, admission to the fellowship of scholars. It is also the means whereby you polish and refine your skills so that you may go on to work which has meaning, interest, and intellectual stimulation for you. Many candidates, in a fine frenzy of ambition, set off on a sea of research in a cockleshell and drown in the attempt. You would be better advised to swim the length of the pool with even strokes, complete coordination, and speed. Four questions to pose to yourself may serve as life preservers:

1. Can I do it in the time I have?
2. Do I have the money to underwrite the costs which will be incurred?
3. Do I have the knowledge and skill to do the job well?
4. Are the materials — books, monographs, journals, dissertations, abstracts, specimens (animal, vegetable, or mineral) — and consultants available?

Selecting a Sponsor [i]

Whether you need one sponsor or a whole covey, set your sights on obtaining the guidance of at least one sympathetic, knowledgeable, conscientious person. If you cannot ask directly without prejudicing the professor you want, be devious and discover whether he is near retirement or planning a sabbatical. If you do not know his work habits, use the student grapevine to learn whether he is one of those affable characters who always say "yes" but are rarely to be found for consultation. Inquire about the rapidity with which he returns materials and whether he just skims or really reads and comments upon what is submitted to him. These are not cynical remarks; they are an attempt to help you deal with reality. Try to determine whether he is producing a book; or absorbed in a research project of his own; or is one of those people who are in great demand as advisors. All of those activities might indicate that he is a great scholar, but they also indicate that he may not be around when you need him most. If you need more than one sponsor, he might do as a second or third. Your major sponsor (chairman) should be someone willing to invest almost as much time and energy as you will have to devote.

Approach him with as sharply defined a topic as possible. Your previous drafts and discussions should have helped you to refine and polish the topic considerably. If you have a firm grip on the subject, it will be easier to

---

[i] Once again, the sequence, detail, and administrative red tape may vary. The step-by-step procedures described, whether actually required of you or engaged in for reasons of self-preservation, should prove useful.

solicit his sponsorship, as well as to deal with alterations in purpose or scope he may suggest.

If he is most of the things the previous discourse implies, he is the man for you. Once he has acquiesced, should you need other sponsors, ask him for suggestions. If he recommends a professor with whom you have had a profitable experience, his recommendation may make acceptance more likely. If he suggests someone with whom you have had an adverse experience, but not a disastrous one, it might be worthwhile to visit with that professor and see if the rift is remediable. If he refers you to someone with whom you *know* you cannot work, say so.

It is foolhardy to start your dissertation plan without the complete *and official* commitment of a chairman. It is even more advantageous to have the counsel of your entire committee. If you have only the chairman, get the rest before you are halfway through the development of the plan.

Occasionally a sponsor will direct that you submit only a completed plan for comment. That same person may also refuse to read your dissertation chapter by chapter. Either get him to change his routine, or do not ask him to serve. You will want every one of your sponsors to read and comment on each part of the proposal and each chapter of the dissertation as you write them. This procedure is insurance against compounding your errors. A felicitous regimen is to provide each member with a different colored pen and to circulate one copy; you will have all comments and suggestions for emendation on it and each of them will have the opportunity to see the direction taken by the others.

The Dissertation Proposal[i]

A carefully conceived, well-written, and thoughtfully designed dissertation proposal can and should save infinite wear and tear on your psyche, feet, eyes, and stomach lining. A good proposal will *not* write your dissertation for you but will make it easier for you to write.

The Statement of the Problem

The *most* important part of this exercise is the statement of your problem. Some departments require an introductory statement. If so, write it. Whether mandated or not, the statement of the problem itself should be written with such clarity and in such logical, sequential fashion that it may

---

[i] Sometimes called an "Outline," an inadequate description; or a "Research Design," a pretentious description. The label may be dictated by the institution in which you are doing your graduate study. It is unimportant. What is important is the process for developing what should be the itinerary and guide for your dissertation, and a solace to you in disheartening hours.

stand on its own merits. If so done, it should indicate not only the problem for which you seek a solution, but also the steps whereby you plan to find that solution.

Example 1. The researcher plans to survey the critical literature on Edgar Allan Poe's "The Raven"; to examine Poe's original manuscript with his corrections and emendations; and to evaluate "The Raven" in the light of both the "old" and the "new" literary criticism.

Example 2. The purpose of the researcher is to write a brief history of the development of the language laboratory method of instruction and to compare the efficacy of the "traditional" method with the language laboratory method[i] in the teaching of French to college freshmen.

The Subproblems

As you can see, neither one of the subjects is "earthshaking," but there is no question left as to what the researcher intends. In addition, he has specified the steps he means to take and the order in which he means to take them.

Those steps constitute his subproblems. They may be posed in interrogatory form or stated in infinitive form. They should be separated from the body of the major statement.

1. To survey the critical literature on Edgar Allan Poe's "The Raven."
2. To examine Poe's original manuscript with his corrections and emendations.
3. To evaluate "The Raven" in the light of both the "old" and the "new" literary criticism.

The major statement and the separately stated subproblems constitute your contract with yourself, your sponsors, and the scholarly world.

Definitions

You cannot know now all of the terms you will use in your dissertation which may require definition. The same applies to your proposal. Under this heading, immediately define those terms you are certain you will use. Add what is necessary for the proposal as you proceed. You may use all, some, or none of them in the dissertation. You may have to add some for it.

Given the two examples of subjects, it is clear that you would define "old" and "new" criticism for Example 1, and "traditional" for Example 2. You might also want to define what you mean by "language laboratory program," since there are several.

---

[i] See "Abbreviations," Chapter II, 18.

A rough gauge of what should or should not be defined and the type of definition most suitable follows:

1. Do not define the obvious, *e.g.*, "freshmen" in Example 2.
2. Define those terms which, though they may be common parlance, have a special meaning or are differently used in your discipline. Even when a definition is similar, there may be special nuances. The engineer and the musician both use the infinitive "to compose," but what each means by "composition" has varying hues. Another example of fine shading is the word "culture." Refinements of it are to be found in, *e.g.*, anthropology, biology and the production of pearls. In another era, it also meant possession of the social graces.
3. Some disciplines have created a "special language." Such terminology, where truly exotic, should be defined. Unfamiliar terms, *e.g.*, Latin names for flowers which have "everyday names," should be defined. This applies as well to terms familiar in one discipline and borrowed and transformed by another discipline. When a dentist explores, he uses an instrument of torture; when you, as a reseacher, explore, it may be painful to you, but not to anyone else.
4. Define only what is absolutely necessary and do so precisely. Wherever possible, use an authoritative source and document (footnote) your definitions. If no other source is available, use the very best dictionary you can find. Many disciplines have their own dictionaries or glossaries of special terms.
5. Occasionally no authoritative definition is exactly what you had in mind. Find one or two such definitions, cite them, and then, using the best of each, create your own definition. This procedure should be used sparingly and only when you may honestly justify adding to our already cluttered language.
6. Complicated, abstruse, lengthy definitions, such as those requiring extensive examples in mathematics or physics, should be placed in an appendix. Simplifications of each, for the enlightenment of laymen, may be placed in the definitions section.

Limitations[i]

Sometimes the very title of your topic indicates a limitation; sometimes the subjects you have chosen constitute a limitation.

In Example 1, you have "agreed" to review the critical literature on Edgar Allan Poe. There is a large body of critical literature on Poe in

---

[i] This section is sometimes labeled "Delimitations." The title "Limitations" encompasses that idea. If your department insists on the former, do not waste your substance arguing on such a minor matter.

French but, if you do not read French with ease, you probably should have a limitation statement.

1. Only the critical literature written in English will be studied.

If you have in mind certain notable critics, you might wish to limit yourself.

2. Among the critics to be consulted, special reference will be made to Lionel Trilling and Alfred Kazin, although a general survey is intended.

For Example 2, you should either specify, in the major statement, what you mean by college freshmen or provide a limitation.

1. Only freshmen in junior colleges will be used.

or

1. Subjects will be drawn from four-year, liberal arts colleges in the Greater New York geographical area, *i.e.*, New York City, Long Island, Westchester, and New Jersey.

If the language laboratory method you are to use is a new and complex one, you might provide a statement of limitation rather than a definition.

2. The language laboratory method designed and tested at Utopia College during the academic years 1969-1970 and 1970-1971 will be used.

You will expand that statement when you are dealing with your method.

When a particular time span is indigenous to the problem to be studied, that, too, should have a limitation statement.

1. The period of time from 1682, when William Penn took possession of his "country," Pennsylvania, to 1755, when the Academy and College of Philadelphia was transformed into the University of Pennsylvania, will be studied.

Note that a justification was given in the last limitation. Some departments require it. Whether you must include it in the proposal or not, you should be prepared with a rationale for each limitation you impose. Incidentally, using a particular source because it is only ten minutes away from your house is not good enough!

Hypotheses

Some departments require that hypotheses be stated early in the proposal. You cannot pull them out of the air to satisfy some administrative fetish! Obviously you would not have chosen the topic if you had not thought that you might come up with some answer or answers. However, in order to protect the research against your own bias, your hunches should *not* be used as hypotheses. Every hypothesis may have some of the elements of a "guess," but it should be an informed guess.

1. Do not include hypotheses except where they are necessary and appropriate. If they are mandated by your department, see "4," below.
2. Research in aesthetics, history, literary criticism, and other subjects may not require hypotheses in the dissertation proposal. In many instances, the hypotheses emerge as a product of the research itself.
3. Research in science and almost all experimental research has hypotheses built in.
4. When hypotheses are necessary and appropriate, they should be developed as you formulate the method. You may then slot them into your final copy in whatever sequence your department requires.

The Need for the Study[i]

If you have done all of your preliminary research homework, this section should just roll off your typewriter. You had better be convinced that there is a genuine need for the study before you try to sell the idea to anyone else. If you are not convinced, no sales pitch will work.

This section should be a *brief* exercise in rhetoric, *i.e.*, persuasion. It is better to promise less and deliver more.

Suppose the following situation: It is 8:00 A.M. in a suburb. A harried housewife has three children to get dressed, breakfasted, and off to the car pool for school; her husband is a commuter, a late riser, wants his coffee hot and his toast cool; and she has a cake for that afternoon's church sale in the oven. You are selling vacuum cleaners and have just rung the bell. She tears to the door and opens it. Her expression tells you that it will close immediately. You stick your foot in the door and look anxious. She says, "You have exactly three minutes to do your spiel."

Keep that housewife in mind and select the most apt, cogent and impressive arguments. Have a closing sentence or paragraph in which you tie all of the arguments together, stating clearly what you hope your research will produce. Be direct, lucid, and discriminating. Don't embellish! Don't waste that woman's time!

Related Literature

There are multifarious purposes for this section. It should demonstrate

---

[i] Some departments prefer the title "The Significance of the Study." Not only is it pretentious, but it may also commit you to producing an extravaganza well beyond the potential of the topic and you. If, when the dissertation is completed, it really is a significant contribution to knowledge, let the scholarly world have the pleasure of being surprised. It may be a unique experience for them.

that you have acquired as much mastery of the literature in your field as is consonant with your academic status and stage of scholarly development; reveal your familiarity with the books, monographs, abstracts, journals, studies, and dissertations apposite to your topic; display your acquaintance with both the classical literature and the most current reports on your subject; illustrate your ability to select that which is most important and your skill in digesting and synthesizing complex data; and assure that you are able to communicate ideas succinctly and in English.

A prefatory statement may aid the reader.

For Example 1. The literature pertinent to the proposed study may be subsumed under the following headings: Critical Literature on Poe, Both "Old" and "New"; "The Raven" and Poe's Corpus of Poetry; "The New Criticism"; and "Approaches to the Study of Poe."

For Example 2. The literature to be discussed will deal with the historical material on language learning; the evolution of the traditional method of teaching languages, especially French; the development of the language laboratory method of instruction; and experimental studies of language learning.

Some departments require a section entitled "Theoretical Design," or "Conceptual Framework" or "Methodological Rationale." If you are so constrained, do so. If you are not obligated to do a separate section with a highfalutin title, and if your proposed research has a full-blown theory as its base, the theory surely has been the subject of one or more studies.

For Example 1. You would deal with theory in the sections on literary criticism and approaches to the study of Poe.

For Example 2. You would deal with theory in the sections on the traditional and language laboratory methods and experimental research.

In addition, your essay on related literature should provide support from the scholarly literature for the arguments you presented in rhetorical form in "The Need for the Study."

Avoid undue use of lengthy quotations.[i] If you have found a study which you consider poorly conceived and even more poorly executed, do not damn it or gloat. Use an example from it, in the author's own words, which will reveal your acuity and will permit the reader to recognize that you have spotted the flaws. After you have your degree, you can write a diatribe for one of the learned journals and hang the other researcher by his thumbs.

---

[i] See all references to quotations in the Index, and, especially, material in Chapter VII, 68–69.

Organize your material! If there are four papers, all of which are studies of the same or related topics, write on the most interesting or expert and refer the reader to the others in a footnote, as follows:

Horst Lovewell[1] studied Eustace Tilley's years of glory and found that, though the number of his readers has declined, he is still popular with the literati.[2]

---

[1] Horst Lovewell, *Eustace Tilley, A Study of the Literary Circles of the Pre and Post World War I Period*, New York: D. Parker, Inc., 1932.

[2] See also, Arthur Marx, *The Square Table at the Comanche*, Boston: Keen and Witty, Inc., 1936, 18-60; Richard Bentley, "A Bunch of the Boys Were Whooping It Up," *The Pacific*, January, 1940, XXII:1, 25, 28-30; and Archimedes Wolport, *Opening Nights and Post-Mortems at the Comanche*, New York: Sheridan and Sherwood, 1942, *passim*.

Pull together all of the material which deals with a theme, a technique, or a theory similar or related to some facet or the whole of your thesis. Do not write in hiccough-like spurts. Revolve your comment on the literature about each focus, and demonstrate the connection between the literature you are surveying and your research. Do *not* belabor the importance of your topic or exaggerate the contribution it will make to your field.

The Method[i]

This is the most important part of your proposal and your dissertation. Whether your study is to be historical, exploratory, descriptive, aesthetic, experimental, philosophical, scientific, critical, or mathematical,[ii] you must use one or more methods of research. If you do not have a firm grip on it or them, quit now!

No matter which method of research you elect, the clarity and precision (those words necessarily recur) with which you demonstrate your knowledge of its use will not only impress your readers, but will also reinforce the technique for you. If some element of the research eludes you, learn it! The experts who will review your proposal will not easily be fooled.

Describe the Method: If you are using a classical method of research throughout, you may wish to write a general introduction in which you describe that method in full. Some of the source material for whatever method you are using surely will have been discussed in your section on related literature. It is legitimate to cross-reference within your proposal, but you should have saved the most important information for this section.

If each subproblem requires the use of a different technique, describe it as a concomitant of your exposition for that subproblem.

For an experimental study in which warm bodies are to be used, even

---

[i] Some departments use the title "Methodology," which is inaccurate and ostentatious.

[ii] See William Shakespeare, *Hamlet*, II:ii, 401-407.

though you may have described them under "Limitations," you should write a paragraph or two about the type, source, characteristics, and any other important data about both your experimental and control groups.

If your sources are not living beings but printed matter of any kind, imagine that each piece of material you are using is a person to be interviewed. Pose questions to it to elicit the apposite information, just as you would in educing data from a human expert.[i]

Describe Your Instruments: When particular instruments, schedules, or questionnaires are to be used, provide a descriptive section about them. This also applies to the use of particular statistical manipulations, computer programs, or languages. Shore up your choice of instruments and manipulative devices by citing reliability and validity figures as supplied by the initiators and other experimenters. Remember, too, that at your final defense, you may be asked to explain why you chose these tools rather than some others.

An instrument of your own devising must be tested in advance of its use in your dissertation. The pilot study or studies you will have done should be reported, and the means you used to establish reliability and validity, with the results — specific figures — should be included.[ii] Again, some of this may have been covered under related literature, but the significant material should have been saved for this section.

Even though you should strive mightily throughout the writing of your proposal for lucid, economic language, do not sacrifice an iota of precision in the method section. If you must condense, edit, and shear, do it elsewhere.

Bibliography [iii]

The method section should be followed by a bibliography. It is either "Tentative Bibliography" or "Preliminary Bibliography" or "Suggested Bibliography" or "Chief Sources," whichever appeals to you. Every book, article, dissertation, report, or abstract[iv] you have mentioned should be included with complete publishing information. Every book, article, dissertation, report, or abstract you think you may read or should read should be included with complete publishing information. The bibliography for your

---

[i] If interviewing is a part of your method, be sure that you have studied the techniques and recognize the questionable aspects of relying on some person's (persons') memory, opinion, bias, etc.

[ii] Although you may have had many courses in experimental research, statistics and computer science, consult the appropriate professors and read anything they recommend to strengthen your knowledge and skill. Taste in texts and computer languages varies so it would be foolhardy to suggest any one source.

[iii] See Chapter V.

[iv] Abstracts may be cited in the proposal; the full document should have been read for the dissertation.

dissertation, itself, may be quite different from this one. You will, unquestionably, find other sources to study before your travail is over. Some of the items you have listed in this bibliography may prove inadequate, inappropriate, or incompetent.

The dissertation proposal bibliography is subject to the same suggestions about format described in Chapter V. If no clear divisions emerge, it is acceptable for this bibliography to be presented in one straight listing, alphabetical by author's surname.

Appendixes [i]

Appendixes should follow the bibliography.

Both in your section on instruments and manipulations and in the separate discourses for each subproblem, if the materials are complex and lengthy, provide an example of each in the text. Put the complete document(s) in an appendix or appendixes.

Curriculum Vitae [ii]

Some departments require a *curriculum vitae* at the end of the proposal. Follow the dictates of your particular institution. If needed, it should include your previous education, from college on, both degree programs and any other study; your professional experience(s); a listing of those courses completed most nearly related to your study; any honors which may have been conferred on you, *e.g.*, academic scholarships, fellowships, degrees conferred *cum, magna cum* or *summa cum laude;* memberships in learned and professional societies; and publication of professional articles or books.

Title

Many candidates waste precious hours in advance of writing the proposal by composing fetching titles. Don't! When the proposal is completed, you will *know* what the title should be. Be certain that it is completely descriptive of what you plan, yet avoid tedious length.

Sample Catalogue for Dissertation Proposal [iii]

Introduction +
The Statement of the Problem
Subproblems

---

[i] See the reference to these under "Definitions," 80–81.

[ii] Sometimes called "Personal Data Sheet."

[iii] This symbol + indicates that the section is optional.

Definitions +
Limitations +
Hypotheses +
The Need for the Study
Related Literature
The Method
   General Introduction +
   Subjects +
   Instruments +
   Statistical Manipulations +
   Subproblems — each restated and each provided with full description of method
Bibliography
Appendix (Appendixes) +
Curriculum Vitae +

It would be wise to provide such a catalogue, with page references, at the beginning of your proposal. Note that it has not been called a "Table of Contents." This is just a map. Your dissertation will be a book and merits a complete guide to its contents.

Onward and Upward

If you have done all of the work required to write the kind of proposal described herein, you will have a reliable, detailed blueprint for the conduct of your research and the writing of your dissertation. You will also have acquired additional skill in expressing your ideas and techniques with precision and clarity.

There is no rule that requires a term paper or a thesis to be dull, nor does a dissertation have to be boring to be scholarly. Scholarly writing may have as its impetus the researcher's passion for a particular subject, but the pursuit and presentation thereof must be conducted with infinite care for validity, reliability, and credibility.

CHAPTER IX
Foreign Words and Abbreviations

Words in Other Languages

In a printed book, words in a language other than English are in italics. If you have at your command a typewriter with changeable type faces and one of those faces is italics, you may italicize. Most people are limited to the use of pica, elite, or executive type.

Rule. Words from a language other than English, which would have been set in italics in print, should be underscored in a typed manuscript. As is customary, there is an exception to this rule.

Exception. The use of a word which had its origins in a language other than English but which is now an accepted word in the English language negates the rule for italics. The most notable example is the abbreviation "etc." That symbol is now an integral part of the English language. It is important to know that "etc." is an abbreviation of two words: *et* = and, *cetera* = others. This is the same *et* in the abbreviation *et al.* Take note that it is a complete word, not an abbreviation; therefore *et* does not require a period after it. Since *al.* is an abbreviation for *alii*, others, it requires a period.

Rule. The only acceptable abbreviation of *et cetera* is "etc." It should *never*, for obvious reasons, be preceded by "and."

There are a number of abbreviations which are in constant use in scholarly writing. Most are from the Latin, some are French or Greek or German. Bearing in mind the strongly stated *exception*, above, they require italicizing, *i.e.*, underscoring. The following list is as precise — and as concise — as possible. When a word or abbreviation is not italicized, it follows that it is not to be underscored.

Rule. When any one of these words or abbreviations is the first word in a footnote, it must have an initial capital.

89

Abbreviation & Word	Meaning	Explanation
anon. anonymous	author unknown	
c. *circa*	about	Used in citing doubtful dates in history.
ca. *circa*	about	Used in this form in narrative.
©	copyright	
cf. *confer*	compare	
ed., eds.	editor, editors	
et al. *et alii et aliae*	and others	The "others" usually refers to people.
et passim	and here and there	Used when citing nonsequential pagination. Follows an actual citation of a page, *e.g.*, 9, *et passim*. See also, *passim* below.
et seq. et sequens, sequentia	and the following	The pages that follow.
e.g. *exempli gratia*	for example	Not to be confused with *i.e.*, below.
f. *folio*	folio size	
ff. *folios*	several sheets of folio size	Also used to indicate "pages following."
ibid. ibidem	Alone, it means "in the same place of the work," as cited immediately above. When followed by a page number or numbers, it means in the work cited immediately above, *but on a different page or pages*.	
i.e., id est	that is	
in re	in the matter of	
loc. cit. loco citato	In the same passage, in the work, on the same page or pages of the same edition, by the same publisher and author previously cited.	
N.B. *nota bene*	note well, take notice	
n.d.	no date of publication	
n.n.	no name	
n.p.	no place of publication	

Foreign Words and Abbreviations / 91

Abbreviation & Word	*Meaning*	*Explanation*
op. cit. opere citato	The work cited, even the author, publisher, and date, but not the same page.	
p., pp.	page(s)	Do *not* capitalize.
passim	here and there	Used when reference has been made to an idea which occurs in various forms and places in a book, article, etc.
per se	by itself, of itself	
pseud.	pseudonym	Equivalent to a pen name.
q.v. quod vide	which see	
sic[i]	thus	Indicates that it is the way you found it and you know there is something wrong. Place in square brackets.
trans.	translator, or translated by	
v. (not underscored)	toward, opposite,	In legal citations, use v. and italicize the names of the litigants. In narrative, use *vs.*
vs. versus	against	
vide ante	see the preceding	
vide infra	see below or the following	
vide supra	see above	
viz. videlicet	that is to say, namely, to wit	

---

[i] If you are dealing with material which uses unfamiliar forms consistently, you should provide a footnote early in the manuscript indicating this atypical condition. If you do not provide the note, you will be *sic*-ing all over the place. Use *sic* with discretion.

Abbreviations Lists

If you are using a variety of esoteric sources, such as highly specialized journals in a particular field, and if there are standard abbreviations for those journals, spell out the entire title the first time you cite the journal and use the abbreviation thereafter. For example, Modern Language Association journal: MLA. However, to assure appropriate reference information to the reader, list the abbreviations in one column and the complete title opposite in another column in an appendix.

You may also list abbreviations of your sources when they are: 1) organizations with complex titles for which there are standard abbreviations, 2) organizations with complex titles for which you used sets of initial letters, or 3) not so complex titles but in such constant use that abbreviation seems advisable.

Examples

Abbreviation	*Title*
B.L.	Bodleian Library
B.M.	British Museum
M.L.	Morgan Library
NIMH	National Institute of Mental Health

Comment. Try to avoid becoming obsessed with initial letter designations. If you use them too freely, you will confuse the reader and irritate him.

When you are using works with exceedingly long titles and will have to use them over and over again, you might well establish abbreviations for those works and put them in your abbreviations list.

Comment. Abbreviations lists may be placed immediately after the table of contents or in an appendix. Regardless of place, the first time you use a title, spell it out in full. Thereafter you may use the abbreviation or initial letter designations.

CHAPTER X
Foreword, Acknowledgments, Table of Contents, Abbreviations

Although the subjects to be discussed in this chapter usually appear at the beginning of a thesis or dissertation and, occasionally, of a major term paper, in actuality they should be written last. Hence their position in this Handbook.

Foreword

The Foreword is sometimes called "Preface" or "Introduction." Its purpose is to inform the reader of what you intended to do. It is placed *before* the table of contents, but it is listed *in* the table of contents. Since the title page of your work is page i, and the copyright is page ii, the Foreword will be page iii.

Rule. Pagination for the material which precedes the first page of the first chapter is in lower-case Roman numerals and appears ½″ from the *bottom* of the page, in the center.

Acknowledgments

An acknowledgment section rarely appears in a term paper. If the writer of a term paper has a genuine debt to a particular person who provided him with guidance or material, he might acknowledge his gratitude in a footnote on the first page.

Custom has dictated that the writer of a thesis or a dissertation express thanks to his sponsor or sponsors and to any other person who lent him counsel and encouragement. This frequently includes patient wives, husbands, and children, and should include librarians. Unfortunately, even when sponsors have been of no help at all, credit is expected!

Another purpose for this section is to acknowledge special permission granted by various publishers and publications for the use of material in the thesis or dissertation. Such permission should have been obtained in writing, and care must be taken to cite each publisher in the form dictated in the letter of permission.

It is possible and acceptable to combine the content of the Foreword and Acknowledgments in one section.

Table of Contents

Since it is not customary for a thesis or a dissertation to have an index, the Table of Contents should be as informative and detailed as possible. The first page is treated as though it were the first page of a chapter with a two-inch margin at the top. The title is centered and in capital letters. All specified margins are maintained and subsequent pages have only a one-inch margin at the top. Titles and pages not only of chapters, heads and subheads should be listed, but also of appendixes and lists of tables, figures, illustrations, etc. The lists follow immediately after the Table of Contents, each as a separate section.

Abbreviations

Should you decide to use a list of abbreviations, it would follow immediately after the table of contents or the lists of illustrations. It, too, would appear in the table of contents with its appropriate page.

[SAMPLE[i]]

TABLE OF CONTENTS

	Page
Foreword	iii
Acknowledgments	v
List of Tables	x
List of Figures	x
List of Pictures	xi
List of Reproductions of Paintings	xii
I. John Locke	1
The Protean John Locke	1
The Purpose of This Researcher	5
Locke's Life	8
Locke's Time	44
The Matter of "Influence"	49

---

[i] See also the Table of Contents for this *Handbook*.

TABLE OF CONTENTS (continued)

	Page
II. John Locke's Educational Theory	61
The Educational Theory Screen	61
Guide to the Composition of the "Screen"	61
The Text	61
The Documentation	63
The "Screen"	66
Aim	69
Content-Purpose	93
Method	159
Analysis of the "Screen"	230
Tutorial *vs.* Public School and University Education	231
The Education of Girls	236
"Child Psychology," "Learning Theory" and	
"Methodology"	238
Individual Differences	238
Early Influences	238
Attention Span	239
Emulation	240
"Blocks," Habits, "Conditioning"	241
Senses, Experience, Memory	242
"Faculty"	243
Discipline, Personality and Character Development	244
"Readiness" and "Transfer"	248
Curiosity	249
"Interest and Motivation"	249
"Learning Process": "Integrated-Correlated-	
Sequential Study"	250
Content	251
Aim	252
Recent Instances	253
. . . .[i]	
Bibliography	662
Appendix A John Locke and the "Founding Fathers"	670
Appendix B The Strange "Case" of Edward Clarke, Jr.,	
Attending Physician: John Locke, Gent.	680

---

[i] Indicates that a considerable portion of the material has been omitted.

Appendixes

Appendix A: Singular and Plural Forms

Singular	Plural	Meaning
art.	arts.	article, articles
Chap.	Chaps.	Chapter, Chapters
col.	cols.	column, columns
ed.	eds.	edition, editions
ed.	eds.	edited by, editor; editors
Fig.	Figs.	figure, figures
l.	ll.	line, lines
MS	MSS	manuscript, manuscripts
n.	nn.	note, notes
		footnote, footnotes
no.	nos.	number, numbers
opus	opera	work, works
p.	pp.	page, pages
par.	pars.	paragraph paragraphs
pt.	pts.	part, parts
sec.	secs.	section, sections
vs.	vss.	verse, verses
vol.	vols.	volume, volumes

* * * * * * * * * * * * * * *

consensus	consensuses	agreement in matters of opinion[i]
criterion (is)	criteria (are)	a means for judging
curriculum (is)	curricula (are)	(Latin: race course) a course of study

---

[i] The phrase "consensus of opinion" is obviously a redundancy.

Singular	Plural	Meaning
datum (is)	data (are)	something given as a fact upon which an inference may be based
dictum (is)[i]	dicta (are)	an authoritative statement
stratum (is)	strata (are)	a category viewed as occupying a level in an hierarchy

Comment. These are merely examples. Check your use of singular and plural forms and be sure that your verbs agree in number.

Appendix B: Books on Usage and Useful Books

Anderson, M. D. *Book Indexing.* Cambridge: At the University Press, 1971.
Bartlett's *Familiar Quotations.* 15th and 125th Anniversary ed. Rev., enlarged and ed. by Bartlett, John. Boston: Little Brown Co., 1980.
Barzun, Jacques. *On Writing, Editing and Publishing Essays, Explicative and Hortatory.* Chicago: University of Chicago Press, 1971.
Bernstein, Theodore M. *The Careful Writer, A Modern Guide to English Usage.* New York: Atheneum, 1977.
──────. *Reverse Dictionary.* With the collaboration of Wagner, Jane. New York: Quadrangle/The New York Times Book Co., 1977.
Beveridge, W. I. B. *The Art of Scientific Investigation.* New York: Vintage Books, A Division of Random House, 1969.
Carroll, David. *The Dictionary of Foreign Terms in the English Language.* New York: Hawthorn Books, Inc. Publishers, 1973.
Collins, F. Howard. *Authors' and Printers' Dictionary.* 10th ed. London: Oxford University Press, 1971.
Dictionary of American Biography. vols. 17. New York: Scribner's, 1927 and supplements.
Dictionary of National Biography. vols. 22. Oxford and London: Oxford University Press, 1917 and supplements.
Fowler, Henry W. *A Dictionary of Modern English Usage.* 2nd ed. Rev. by Gowers, Sir Ernest. New York: Oxford University Press, 1965.
Gallagher, Ruth Gleeson and Calvin, James. *Words Most Often Misspelled and Mispronounced.* New York: Pocket Books, 1972.

---

[i] The use of this word in legal matters, *e.g.*, in the term *obiter dictum*, is different. For legal use, it means a judicial opinion on a point other than the precise issue involved in a case.

Gowers, Sir Ernest. *The Complete Plain Words.* Rev. by Fraser, Sir Bruce. London: Her Majesty's Stationery Office, 1973.
Mawson, C. O. Sylvester. *Dictionary of Foreign Terms.* 2nd ed. Rev. and updated by Berlitz, Charles. New York: Barnes & Noble Books, A Division of Harper and Row Publishers, 1979.
Newman, Edwin. *On Language: Strictly Speaking & A Civil Tongue.* New York: Warner Books, 1980.
Oxford Dictionary for Writers and Editors. London: Oxford University Press, 1981.
Oxford Dictionary of Quotations. 3rd ed. London: Oxford University Press, 1979.
Oxford English Dictionary. The Compact Edition. vols. 2. London: Oxford University Press, 1971.
Strunk, William, Jr. and White E. B. *The Elements of Style.* with Index. 3rd ed. New York: The Macmillan Co., 1979.
van Leunen, Mary-Claire, *A Handbook for Scholars.* New York: Alfred A. Knopf, 1978.
Webster's New Biographical Dictionary. Springfield, Mass.: Merriam-Webster Inc. Publishers, 1983.
Webster's New International Dictionary of the English Language. Unabridged. 2nd ed. Springfield, Mass.: G. & C. Merriam Company Publishers, 1960.
Weihofen, Henry. *Legal Writing Style.* 2nd ed. St. Paul, Minn.: West Publishing Co., 1980.
Zinsser, William. *On Writing Well: An Informal Guide to Writing Non-Fiction.* 2nd ed. New York: Harper & Row, 1980.
_____. *Writing with a Word Processor.* New York: Harper and Row, 1983.

INDEX

Numbers refer to pages.
Footnote references include page and footnote number, e.g., 86 n.i.

Abbreviations: etc. 89; foreign language 89–92; *Ibid.* 40; in footnotes 32; in lengthy names 32; line or lines 35; lists or sections of 49 n.i.; 92, 94; missing information in footnotes 39; of names, organizations, titles 18, 39, 92; of singular and plural forms 96, 97; parenthetical indication of 15; scholarly 89, 91; *sic* 91 n.i.

Abstracts, Digests, Syntheses: *Dissertation Abstracts* 76; in footnotes 20; in related literature 84; proscription of use 19–20; 86 n.i.

Acknowledgments 93–94

Anthology: bibliography entry 48; in footnotes 32–33, 38, 44.

Appendix(es) abbreviations 92; contents of 87; in dissertation 87; in term paper 72; pagination 22.

Art 45, 52, 60–61.

Article 14, 33.

Article(s): direct quotation from 14; in bibliography 47; in footnotes 2, 31–32, 38, 43.

Author(s): as reviewer 2; committee as author 39, 46; copyright holder 1, 31; in footnotes 31–33; more than one book by same author 48; multiple authors 32–33, 38–39, 48–49; no author 39, 44, 46; one author revised by another 43; organization as author 39, 46; original author of classic 35.

Bias 68.

Bibliography: abbreviations section 49 n.i; alphabetical listing 46; art 45, 52; assembling 72; bar for second citation of same author 48; charts 52; classification within 45–46; complete page references for 26; entries 46–51 — anthology 48, article 47, book 46–47, chapter 47, compilation 48, essay 47, journal 47, letters 51, magazine 47, more than one book by same author 48, multiple authors 48–49, music 52, newspaper articles 52, recordings 52; graphs 52; holographs 46, 49; illustrations 45, 52; indenting 46; in dissertation 86–87; issue number 47; letters 41; manuscripts 46, 49, 52; margins 46; missing information 50 n.i; newspaper 52; no enumeration of 49 n.i; organization as author 46; page references — anthology 48, article 47, book 48, chapter in book 47, compilation 48, essay 47, letters 41, pagination 22, photographs 45, 52; separate sections 45, 46; spacing 49; tables 52; title page 49 n.ii; translations, translator 17.

Book(s): bibliography entry 73–74; copyright page 1, 22; direct quotation of 4; editions 25, 34, 42–43; footnote for 32, 44 — anthology 32–33, chapter in 32–33, collection 32–33; footnote repeated by chapter 33; illustrations in 54; reissued 38; report(s) 65; reviews 5, 68; revisions 42–43; title 14; volumes 42–43.

Brackets, bracketed: insert in a quotation 26; in taking notes 4

Brochures, see Journals

Capitalization: articles 14, 33; footnotes 31, 33; *Ibid.* 40; prepositions 14, 33; titles 13–14.

Caricatures, Cartoons, see Photographs.

Cassettes 45, 52.

Cataloguing: cross reference 3, 70; system 45, 87.

Chapter(s): bibliography by chapter content 46; classical 34–35; direct quotation 4; first page 22; footnote numbering within 30; footnoting of 32–33, 44; none in proposals or term papers 23, 38; head 22–23; repeated citations of same work 38; title 4, 23.

Charts: appropriate use 53–54; bibliography 52; captions 58; copyright laws 58; examples 58–59; footnoting of 58–59; legends 58; margins 54; notation 58; numbering 58; placement 54, 56; reduction 56; symbols 58; table of contents 52.

99

Citations, see Footnotes.
Classics 25, 34–35, 44.
Committee As Author, 38, 46.
Computer Retrieval Systems 3.
Conceptual Framework 84.
Copyright: charts 58; Fair Use 27; graphs 58; holder 2, 31; illustrations 58; insignia 22; international 2; laws 1–2; notice 2; page 2–3, 21, 93; permission 2, 31; poetry 27; symbol 22; tables 54.
Cross Reference(s) 3, 70, 85.
Curriculum Vitae 87.

Datrix 76.
Delimitations 81–82.
Dialogue 28–29.
Diction: correctness v, 7–8, 9–12; economy 7–8; editing 72–73; "feel"; and "think" 5, 71–72.
Discrepancies 5–6.
Dissertation Abstracts 76.
Doctoral Dissertation(s): abstracts prohibited 19–20; appendixes 87; availability of material 78; bibliography 86–87; chairman 78–79; citations 2–3, 19; copyright laws 1–2; *curriculum vitae* 87; Datrix 76; definition of terms 80–81; *Dissertation Abstracts* 76; dissertations in process 76; footnoting chapters within 38; in footnotes 19–35, 44; hypotheses 82–83; instruments 86; limitations 77–78, 81–82; method 85–86; money 78; need for the study 83–84; problem statement 79; reading drafts 78–79; related literature 83–85; repeated citations of same work 38; requirements 75, 77 n.ii, 78 n.i; research 75, 76, 85–86; skill 78; sounding board 74; sponsor 74, 77, 78–79; statistics 75–76, 86 n.ii; subproblems 80, 85; table of contents 88; taking notes 2–3; time 78; title 87; topic or subject 74–78 — approval of 76, change of 75–76, 85, competence for 75–76, has it been done 76, express in writing 74, 76, 78–79; uniqueness 77–78.
Documentation, see Footnotes and Bibliography
Draft(s): abstracts, digests 19–20; cutting and pasting 71; editing 71–72; first draft 70–71; footnote enumeration 30; footnoting of 70–71; inserted pages 22; outline 69–70; pagination 22, 71; second draft 71–72; spacing 70–71.

Edit, Edited, Editing 8–9, 70–72.
Edition(s): abridged 66; choosing 67; citation 34; classics 25; footnoting of 42–43; international 2; more than one 2, 66, 69; revisions 42–43.

Editorial, Editor(s): bibliography entry 47; in footnote 32–33; multiple editors 38–39; no editor 39.
Ellipses: beginning of incomplete sentence 25; ending of incomplete sentence 26; in a quotation 25.
Essay(s): bibliography entry 47; footnoting collection of 32–33, 44.

Figures: appropriate use 53–54; bibliography 52; captions 58; copyright laws 58; examples 58–59; footnoting of 58–59; legend 58; margins 54; notation 58; numbering 58; placement of 54, 58–59; reduction 56; symbols 58.
Final Copy, Final Manuscript: abstracts prohibited 19, 20 n.i; dissertation proposal 88; footnote enumeration 30; inserted pages prohibited 22; proofreading 73; writing of 5–7, 72–73.
Footnotes, Footnoting: abbreviation of title 32; abstracts 19–20; anthology 32–33; Arabic numerals 2 n.i, 31, 34–35; article 31–32, 44; bar between footnote and text 30; book 32, 44; capitalization 31, 33; chapter 32–33, 44; charts 58; classics 25, 34–35, 44; digests 19–20; dissertation 35, 44; drafts 70–72; editions 25, 34, 42–43; enumeration 30; essay in collection 32–33, 44; figures 58; first citation 33, 38, 42–43; foreign language 17; graphs 58; group of researchers dealing with single concept 27, 85; *Ibid.* 40; illustrations 58; information needed 2–3; interview 41, 44; issue number 31; lecture notes 41–42, 44; legal 36; letters 41; lower case Roman numerals 2, 31, 34–35; Master's thesis 35, 44; mimeographed paper 35, 44; missing information 39; multiple authors or editors 38–39; newspaper article 42; organization as author or editor 39; page references 32; pamphlet 39, 44; paraphrase 36, 69; phone call 41; photograph 60–61; placement 31; place of publication 37; play 34–35; poetry 27–28; quotations 69; reissued books 43; repeated citations of same work 38, 42–43; revisions 42–43; sequence for — article 31–32, book 32, classics 34–35; series of researchers 27; spacing 22, 30–31, 40, 79; specific edition 34, 69; superior number for 26–27; symbols for 2 n.i; syntheses 19; tables 54; translations, translator 17–18, 25; volume number 31; volumes 42–43; within a chapter 38; within a term paper 38.
Foreign Language 17–18, 89–91.
Foreword, Introduction, Preface 33 n.i, 93.
Form, Format: absence of quotation marks 25–26; citation of poetry 27–28; copyright symbol 22; ellipsis in a quotation 25; heads

23-24; incomplete sentence in a quotation 25; insert in a quotation 26; levels of subheads 23; margins 21; pagination 21-22; quality of paper 21; quotation marks, quotations, ellipses 24; quotation within a quotation 24-25; spacing 22-23; subheads 23-24; superior number 26-27.

Graphs, see Charts and Figures.

Holographs 46.
Hypotheses 82-83.

Ibid. carried over 40; in tables 56; use of 40.
Illustrations: appropriate use 53-54; bibliography 45, 52; captions 58-61; copyright laws 58; date 60-61; footnoting 58-59; margins 54, 61; numbering 60; placement 58, 60; reduction 61; size, *e.g.*, 60.
Indent, Indented 16, 22-23, 24, 25-26, 27, 46.
Index 6.
Instruments 86.
Interview, Interviewing 41, 42, 86 n.i.
Introduction 33, n.i, 93.
Issue Number 31, 47.
Italics: absence in citing Bible 34; absence in citing dissertations, theses, etc. 35; addition of to quotation 18; foreign words 89-91; language other than English 17; presence in citing classics 34; titles 14; underscoring as substitute 17, 31, 32, 47.

Journals, see Article(s).

Learned Journals 84.
Lecture 41-42, 44.
Legal Writing: citations, documentation 36-37.
Letter(s) 26, 41-42, 45, 49.
Librarian(s), Library 63, 65-68, 76.
Limitations 81-82.

Magazine, see Article(s).
Manuscripts 46, 49, 52.
Margins: avoid white space 21; bibliography 46; footnotes 30; for indented quotations 25-26; for page numbers — Arabic 22, lower case Roman 21; maintenance of 71; spacing 71; stipulated 21; tables, charts, graphs, illustrations 54, 56, 61.
Master's Thesis(es): abstracts prohibited 19-20; chairman 78-79; citation of 2; copyright laws 1-2; in footnotes 35, 44; footnoting chapters within 38; notes for 2-4; reading drafts 78-79; repeated citations of same work 78-79; requirements 2; selecting a sponsor 78-79.
Mathematics Papers 31, 53.
Mechanical Preparation 5.
Method, Methodology 85-86.
Methodological Rationale, 84.
Microfiche, Microfilm: citation of 19-20; footnotes in 31; information from 2; University Microfilms 76 n.i; use of 19.
Mimeographed Material 35, 44.
Monograph(s), see Pamphlet.
Music 52.

Need for the Study 83.
Newspaper(s): articles 2; bibliography 82; byline 42; footnoting 32, 42; permission 2; staff writer 42.
Notes: sorting 71; use of in books and journals of science and social science 31.
Number, Numbering, Numbers: enumerated series 16; footnote number 30; footnotes in drafts and final copies 30; identifying abstracts, digests, syntheses 19-20; in footnote 30; in an outline 16-17; note cards 3-4; pages 4, 21-22; punctuation and numbers 16; spell out 17; superior number — with group of researchers for single concept 27, paraphrase 27, quotation 26, series of researchers 27; tables, figures, graphs 53-54, 58.
Numerals: Arabic v n.i, 16, 22, 31, 34-35, 54, 58; forbidden 17; in an outline 16; Roman 1 n.i, 16, 21, 22, 31, 34-35, 54, 93; with tables, charts, graphs, illustrations 53-54, 58, 60.

Organization As Author 39, 46.
Outline: dissertation 79 n.i; form 16; term paper 69-70.

Page, Pages, Pagination: appendix(es) 22; Arabic numerals 22; before text 21-22; bibliography 22, 26, 47; copyright 21-22; drafts 22, 71; first page of chapter 22; in footnotes 30; foreword 93; inserted 22; letters 41; letter transcripts 22; noting 2, 4; pencil 22; placement 21-22, 93; Roman numerals, lower case 21-22, 93; text 22; title page 21, 93; unpaginated 39.
Pamphlet: direct quotation of 4; footnote 44; missing information 39.
Paper 21, 71.
Paraphrase: citation of 4, 37, 69; selective 68-69; superior number for 27.
Parentheses, Parenthetical 15-16.
Permission to Use 1-2, 42.
Personal Data Sheet 87 n.ii.
Personal Pronoun vii, 8.

Photographs, Pictures: appropriate use 56; bibliography 45, 52; copyright laws 58; examples 60–61; margins 54, 61; numbering 60; reduction 61.
Plagiarism: altering author's words 4–5; paraphrasing 5; plagiarizing 5.
Plays 34–35, 44, 69, 85 n.ii.
Plural Forms 96–97.
Poetry 27–28.
Preface(s) 65, 93.
Prepositions in Title 14.
Problem: statement of 79–80; subproblems 80.
Professor(s), see Teacher(s).
Pronouns: use of feminine and masculine v, n.ii.
Proofreading 73.
Proposals, see Drafts and Outlines: abstracts, digests, syntheses cited 19–20; appendix(es) 87; bibliography 86–87; catalogue 87–88; *curriculum vitae* 87; definition of terms 80–81; dissertation proposal footnote enumeration 30; hypotheses 82–83; inserted pages 22; limitations 63–64, 77–78, 81–82, 85–86; method 85–86; need for the study 83, 84; no chapters 23; problem statement 79–80; related literature 83–85, 86; subproblems 80, 85; theses footnote enumeration 30; title 87.
Publication: date 31–32, 39; name 31–32; place 32, 37; publisher 31, 32.
Publisher(s): copyright holder 2, 31; in footnote 32; name 33, 39; organization as publisher 39; permission to cite 2, 94; reissued book 43.
Punctuation: bibliography entry 47; brackets 26; colon 14 — before a quotation 14, in bibliography 47, in footnotes 32, 34–35, with quotation marks 24; comma 14 — in footnotes 31–32, 34–35, with minor series 15, with quotation marks 24; dash(es) 15–16; exclamation point 14 — with quotation marks 24; in footnote for — article 31–32, Bible 34, book 32, classics 34–35, play 34–35, poetry 27–28; *Ibid.* 40; numbers and punctuation 16, 47–48; parentheses 15, 16; period 14 — in ellipses 25, with numbers 16, with quotation marks 24; question mark 16 — with quotation marks 24; semi-colon 14 — with major series 15; single quotation marks 14, 24; slash mark 24, 28 n.i.

Quotation(s): accuracy 33, 69; beginning of sentence 26; beginning of paragraph 26; classics 25; consult original 33; direct 4, 68–69; ellipsis(es) in 25; five or more lines 24; incomplete beginning of sentence 25; incomplete end of sentence 26; indented 24, 26; insert within 26; italics added 18; limiting of 68–69, 84; pages 4; permission for 1; poetry 27–28; spacing 24; superior number at end 26; translated into English 17–18; within narrative 25; within a quotation 14, 24–25.
Quotation Marks: absence thereof 25–26; bibliography 47; in footnotes 31, 35; deleted 24–25; single 14, 24; with colon, 24, 26; comma 24; exclamation point 24; period 24; question mark 24; semi-colon 24; within a quotation 14, 24–25.

Recordings 45, 52.
Related Literature 83–84, 85, 86.
Research, Researcher(s), see Taking Notes: availability of material 78; bias 68 — protect against 82–83; competence in 75–76, 78; current 75; design 79 n.i; early start 63; extent of 63, 67; indexes of 76; library search 66–70; principles of 76; in process 76; instead of personal pronoun 8; popular literature 68; preliminary 63; scope 62–64, 66–67, 77–78, 81–82; sources 63; technique 27, 76, 85–86; vocabulary in historical context 66; work plans 65–70.
Revisions 42–43.

Scholars, Scholarship, Scholarly: diction 18; literature 83–85; paper 88; subheads 23; writing 7, 9.
Scientific Papers 31, 53.
Scientific American 2.
Significance of the Study, 83 n.i.
Singular Forms 96–97.
Slash Marks 28, 40 n.i.
Spacing: bar between text and footnotes 30; bar instead of author's name in bibliography 48; beginning of indented quoted sentence, not paragraph 26; bibliography 46; centering 22–23; chapter heading 23; dialogue 28–29; drafts 70–71; ellipsis(es) 25; footnotes 22, 30–31, 71; heads and subheads 23–24; incomplete beginning of indented quoted sentence 25; incomplete ending of indented quoted material 26; indented quoted paragraph 26; indenting the bibliography 46; poetry 27; quotations 24; text 22; title page 21–22.
Spelling v, 13, 17, 72.
Sponsor 22, 78–79, 93.
Statistics 53, 75–76, 86.
Structure 8–9, 71.
Style: books 97–98; format 21–28; heads and subheads 23; problems v; spacing 22–23.
Subject(s), see Topic(s).
Subproblems 80.

Index / 103

Symbol(s): copyright 22; $ and % 17; figures 58; footnote v n.i; tables 54.
Synthesis(es) 19, 72, 84.

Table of Contents: charts 52; dissertation 88, 94; graphs 52; illustrations 52; sample 94–95; tables 52.
Tables: appropriate use 53; copyright laws 54; division 56; examples 55–57; footnote 54; heading 54; legend 54; margins 54; notation 54; numbering 53–54; placement 54, 58; reduction 56; symbols 54; table of contents 52.
Taking Notes: brackets 4; cataloguing 3–4; copyright notice 3; cross-reference 3, 70; discrimination 4, 69; library search 66–69; note cards 3–4, 69–70; pages 2–4; paraphrase 2–4, 69; quotations — accuracy 4, 68, 69; sorting 70; total information 1–2; underscoring 69; unused 4.
Tapes 45, 51–52.
Teacher(s); idiosyncrasies 62–64; predilections 75; reliability 63; sponsor 78–79.
Telephone Interview 81 n.i.
Term Paper(s): acknowledgments 93; bias 68; change of topic 63; citations in 2; competence 63–64; descriptive sentence or paragraph 65–67, 70, 72; due date 63; early start 64; footnote enumeration 30; footnotes 69, 70, 71, 72; length of 62; margins 21, 71; no chapters 23; number of papers due 63, 72; outline 69–70; pagination 71; paraphrase 69; popular sources 68; procedures 64–70; publication of 2–3; purpose of 65; quotations 68–69; reading rate 63, 67; requirements 62; research for 65–69, scope 62, 67; selection of topic 62–64; self-knowledge 62–64, 67; taking notes 2–4, 68–69, 72; the teacher 62–64; title 64, 72; writing 70–73.
Theme(s), see Subject(s).
Theoretical Design 84.
Theory 84.
Title Page(s) 21–22.
Title(s): article 31; article(s) in 14; book 14; chapter 21; dissertation 87; first word 14; journals 14; preposition(s) in 14; term paper 64, 72.
Topic(s): approval of 76; availability of sources 63, 78; change of 64, 76, 85; dissertation examples 80; express in writing 74, 76, 78–79; familiarity with 63–64; limitation of scope 62, 63–64, 67, 78, 81–82; preliminary research 63; selection 62–64, 75–77; sorting notes by 70; term paper examples 65–67.
Translation(s), Translator(s) 17–18, 34–35.
Typing, see Spacing: bibliography 46, 48; complete manuscript 72–73; copyright symbol 22; dialogue 28–29; footnotes 30–31, 71; margins 21; indented quotations 24–26; name on each page of draft 22; one side of paper 22; paper 21.

Usage: abstracts, digests, syntheses 19–20; abbreviations 18; addition of italics 18; books on 97–98; capitalization 13–14; colon before a quotation 14; diction 7–8, 9–12; economy 7–10; material in language other than English 17–18; numbers and numerals 17; numbers and punctuation 16; outline form 16; paragraph structure 8; parenthetical remarks 15–16; personal pronouns 8; primary citation of person in the text 18–19; punctuation 14–16; sentence structure 8–9; single quotation marks 14, 24; spelling 13; symbols 17; titles 13–14; unnecessary words 5.

Volume(s) 31–32, 34–35, 42–43, 47.

White Space 21.
Word Processor 5.
Writing: dissertation 88; drafts 70–72; economy 7–9; final copy 72–73; organization 85; precision, clarity, lucidity 86; skill or absence thereof 63–64.

Xerox 2, 21, 76, n.i.